THE
HISTORY OF POLPERRO

A FISHING TOWN ON THE SOUTH
COAST OF CORNWALL

BEING A DESCRIPTION OF THE PLACE,
ITS PEOPLE, THEIR MANNERS, CUSTOMS,
MODES OF INDUSTRY, ETC.

BY

JONATHAN COUCH

ILLUSTRATED BY FRANK VARTY

FRANK GRAHAM, *6, Queen's Terrace, Newcastle upon Tyne, 2.*

FIRST PUBLISHED 1871

THIS EDITION 1965

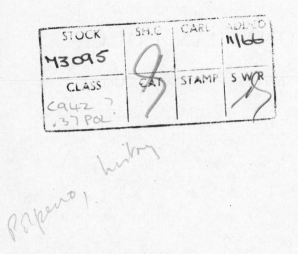
Printed by Howe Brothers (Gateshead) Ltd.

PREFACE

The History of Polperro by Jonathan Couch is a fine example of a local history. Although written over 100 years ago it did not, like so many histories of the nineteenth century, deal only with the landed gentry and the church, but was a true account of the history of the people of Polperro, their work, their customs, and their beliefs.

We have abbreviated the story a little, omitting what we feel might not be of interest to the modern reader and have added a number of illustrations.

At the time when he wrote, old ideas about fairies and witchcraft were still current. Popular superstitions, pastimes, and traditions still survived. The value of Jonathan Couch's history lies in the fact that he preserved this social history for posterity.

CONTENTS

SKETCH OF THE LIFE OF JONATHAN COUCH

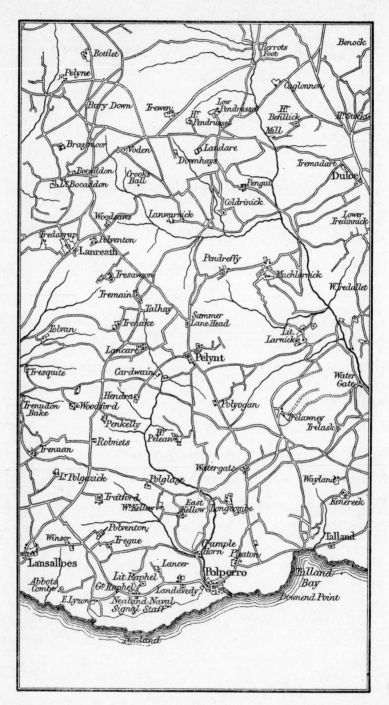

LIFE OF JONATHAN COUCH

Jonathan Couch was born at Polperro on March 15th 1789. Except in the narrow circle of Polperro his family were not of great social importance. Educated first at a Dame's School, and then at a boarding school at Pelynt, he eventually went to the Grammar School at Bodmin. On leaving Bodmin he trained for medicine and finally settled down as a doctor at Polperro where he stayed for the rest of his life. He had early shown a great interest in natural history and he devoted all his spare time to studying and writing about his favourite subject.

His was a very busy life and the amount of his published and unpublished work is very great. As a result of his residing at Polperro he was greatly interested in fishing. He collaborated with Thomas Bewick, the great wood-engraver, on a book about British Fishes which unhappily due to Bewick's death, was never completed. He also assisted with pen and pencil in Yarrell's History of British Fishes. In 1862 he commenced his magnum opus a *History of the Fishes of the British Isles* which was completed in four volumes by 1865.

The fishermen of Polperro materially assisted him in his work especially by obtaining for him specimens fresh from the water. For this reason the figures of fish in his work drawn by himself, are full of colour. "For, as every fisherman knows, the tints which mark them on their coming from sea or river, are to those which they exhibit on the salesman's stall, as the hues of sunset to the monotone of twilight". "The habits of marine animals are confessedly, and from necessity, little known. His unremitting labour was aided by the intelligence of the fishermen, and he gathered an immense amount of information concerning the migrations, times of breeding, food, in short the life of the fishes of British seas and rivers".

The History of Polperro was left by Jonathan Couch in manuscript. It deals with events down to 1856. It was edited by Thomas Quiller Couch and published in 1871. Thomas Q. Couch added a detailed life of the author and made many useful additions to the history.

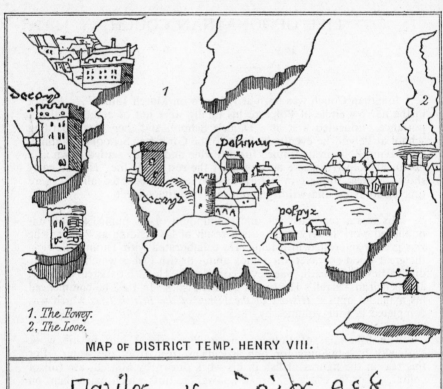

1. The Fowey.
2. The Looe.

MAP OF DISTRICT TEMP. HENRY VIII.

Παυλα εις ᵕοϳα θεᵭ

Δωρεαν ελαβεϳ δω

ϙεαὐδοτε.

Dαϐΐtbǜisʜis gɴoɋsfⲙɪϲɴɪ

KILLIGARTH STONE.

1

DESCRIPTIVE

The earliest notice of the town yet discovered is in Bishop Brantyngham's Register, dated 1392, where mention is made of the chapel of S. Peter de *Porthpyre*. In a deed of the sixth year of Henry V., it is called *Porpere*. A chart of the district made in the reign of Henry VIII., now in the British Museum, and copied by Lysons, gives *Polpyz*, interpreted to mean *fish-pool;* but it may reasonably be supposed that the terminal letter was modified by the engraver, and that the name was meant to be *Polpyr*, for Leland, writing in the same reign, calls it *Poulpirrhe*, *Poulpier*, and *Poulpyrre*. Holingshed mentions a rill between the Fowey and Looe rivers, which he names *Polpir*. Leland says, "From Pontus cross", (Punch's cross, Fowey), " to *Poulpirrhe* about a six miles wher is a little fischar town and a peere, with a very little creke and a broke. There is a crikket betwixt *Poulpirrhe* and Low", (probably Talland sand). "From *Poulpirrhe* to Low creke dry at half ebb a 2 miles". In another place he says, "by East of the haven of Fowey upon a iiii miles ys a smawle creke called *Poul Pier*, and a symple and poore village upon the est side of the same, of fischar men, and the bootes ther fishing by, saved by a peere or key. In the est side also of the *Poulpyrre*, ii miles of, is another creke cawled Loow being but a tyde creke". Leland's description would almost imply that he had no nearer acquaintance with Polperro than he could get in voyaging past it, as he would then only see the simple and poor village which is upon its east side, whilst the western or Lansallos part would be hidden from his view by the Kayne hill.

Carew, in Elizabeth's time, mentions it in the following very descriptive sentence: "A little to the westward from Killigarth the poore harbour and village of Polpera coucheth betweene two steepe hills, where plenty of fish is vented to the fish-drivers, whom we call jowters". Carew's book is full of misprints, but it is probable that in this instance his spelling was correct, as it agrees pretty closely with the present pronunciation; and the oral transmission of a name is generally to be trusted before documentary evidence.

The name has been variously derived from *Pol*, a pool, and *pry*, mud or clay: from Porth para, the sandy port; or has been thought to be purely English, and to mean the pool-pier.

Another name by which the place was sarcastically known was *Polstoggan*, and this was transformed by still more unfriendly neighbours into Polstink, from the smell, so disagreeable to the nostrils of strangers, arising from the offal of fish when it abounded. Stoggan signifies thick or tenacious, such as mud or clay may be. The name *Polstoggan* was never more than satirically used, and is now forgotten, while the Polperro folks had no unapt retort for their neighbours.

Polperro is romantically placed in a deep valley on the south-east of Cornwall, about eighteen miles west of Plymouth, and four miles of Looe.

The vale, or rather *coomb*, in which it is situated, is long and narrow, winding singularly, so that where one hill recedes, the opposite advances to fill up the vacancy; and its steep sides look as if they had been torn asunder by some violent convulsion of nature, and still bore marks of the disruption. At Crumplehorn, a hamlet some three furlongs up the valley, is the confluence of two coombs, each with its attendant rill. Converging, they form the Polperro valley. The sides of the precipitous hills, on either side, are roughened by bare rocks rising tier above tier, or in almost vertical ridges. The junction of the rivulets at Crumplehorn forms a brook, small in summer, but of considerable size and great rapidity in winter, which, running downwards to the harbour, divides the town into two parts. The western half is in the parish of Lansallos, and once formed a part of the manor of Rafiel; the eastern half is in Talland, and belongs to the manor of Killigarth. This brook is sometimes dangerously impetuous from the declivity of the land; for the sea, at our highest tides and storms, rarely flows into it more than four hundred yards above high-water mark. It is crossed by four bridges of the rudest construction and very modern date. At no greater distance than a century back there was in The Green only a narrow bridge for foot passengers, whilst horses and vehicles were compelled to ford the stream, often at a risk. This was, however, enough for the needs of the town; there being at that time only one cart in parish of Lansallos, for drays, dorsals, and crooks were the common modes of conveyance.

The harbour of Polperro, locally termed the *hauen*, opens into the ocean in a south-easternly direction, and runs up into the land a furlong. It is guarded on its western extremity by a natural breakwater, jutting out from the base of the Chapel hill. The *Peak*, as this rocky barrier is named, forms a bold and picturesque object of no ordinary character; its craggy pinnacles rising in two huge masses, to the height of ninety feet. On the eastern side, the mouth of the hauen is bounded by the hill's abrupt descent into the sea, ending in a ledge of irregular wave-worn rocks. The inward sweep of the wave is broken by two piers, both thrown out from the foot of the south-western hill, and built of the blue and red schist of the neighbourhood.

There are a few prominent points worthy of notice in the harbour, of which I shall speak as they occur in a crescentic sweep of it from east to west.

The bold hill descending to the sea on the eastern side of the haven is a portion of the seaward boundary of the manor of Killigarth; it is called the *warren*, and probably was a rabbit preserve when the owner of Killigarth lived there. At present it is a sheep-walk, too steep and rocky for cultivation, except in patches which are taken by the fishermen for the cultivation of potatoes. It dips into the sea by a protruding and elevated cliff named *Dennis ball*. This bears no mark of any ancient work or fortification, as the name might lead us to expect, though perhaps the word *dinas* may have originally meant rather a place of outlook than defence, in confirmation of which the coastguard have taken advantage of the situation for the erection of a signal-staff and watch-house which command a wide extent of sea.

Coming towards the harbour we have a scoop in the cliff called Scilly Cove and *Scilly Cove drang*, neither of these places being particularly remarkable except for their names, which are too nearly related to that of the Scilly Islands to warrant a doubt that their derivation is the same. I do not seek for any deep meaning in the name, but think it taken from the Cornish name of a conger, which is *Syllah*, although I do not know of any special connection between the places and the fish. The word *drang* means a narrow gully, and is only an ancient form of the modern word *throng*, though the former is with us applied rather to a place, than a collection of people.

Proceeding inwards to the town we reach a spot above "yellow rock", once known as "Guns", but now so altered that the name is almost forgotten. It was an earthen battery of four small cannon formed in 1779, when a French fleet cruised off the coast, and was expected to have had designs upon Plymouth. I do not know whether the guns were supplied by the Government, or were merely a local attempt to defend the place against small marauders. Yellow rock, (as it is called, though the colour is reddish), is the first landing place on the Talland side; and near it for many years was the coastguard station.

Consona rocks, (a name now lost), were the ridge of rock next reached, but now covered by a shipwright's yard, built at the beginning of the present century. Near this yard is a free and constant stream of pure water named *Pallace-shute*. The name, it is scarcely necessary to say, is not derived from any building laying claim to even traditionary royalty, but may have reference to an erection near, having some of those characteristics from which even regal residences took their name. It was built in square fashion, with a pent-roof on its four sides, for the curing of pilchards, inclosing a central *court*.

The next object of notice we reach in our sweep of the harbour is the beach, or "strand", inside the old quay. It consists of a layer of coarse gravel, with a substratum of blue clay, in which may be found the trunks of small trees, clearly the alder, their rootlets penetrating into the soil beneath. Further up the coomb where it is thinner, a stratum of sand is found *below it*, containing hazel nuts; but I have not known it penetrated at the "strand", and no remains of animal substances have anywhere been found. It is plainly evident that the alder and hazel grew where the tide now flows, and where these trees are now absent. I explain the fact of their growth in a place now occasionally covered by the sea, by supposing the soil and clay to have slid along the declivity for some distance. Yet still the existence of any sort of trees or bushes growing in such a place must carry our imagination back to a time when no more than the few huts of a fishing village constituted the town of Polperro. What connection have these evidences of a once well-wooded country, now destitute of trees, taken in conjunction with the other marks around

11

our coast both north and south, with the traditional submergence of a large tract of land named Lyonesse, which, with the changes effected by our Saxon conquerers diminished so much the limits of the ancient kingdom of Cornwall? Around our coast from Plymouth to Padstow, along a line almost bare of wood except in rare spots, the storms of winter expose the remains of once mighty forests, now submarine; great boles of trees lying *in situ* as they grew. Traditional and other evidence are so great in proof of the submergence of a large tract of land in old Cornwall that it scarcely a matter of doubt; though the exact period at which it happened, and the quantity of land covered by the ocean, must ever remain uncertain.

Near the strand on the Lansallos side are the "fish scales", or market, where you may often see a busy group of fishermen, clad in Guernsey-frocks, sou'westers, and sea-boots, bargaining, by a sort of auction, with loquacious jowters, *i.e.*, travelling fishmongers, for the contents of the "ocean-smelling osier" (too sweet a term, perhaps, for the brown slimy pannier); or for piles of cod, ling, and conger, too bulky to be so contained.

The old quay is the next stage in our progress. We have no means of ascertaining its age, though, from its name and position, I conclude it to be the same that Leland mentions as existing in his day, or to occupy the same site. It must have been built under the patronage (at least) of the owner of Rafiel, to whom the right of the harbour belonged. The mode of erection of this pier was by parallel walls of solid construction, filled up in the middles by stones and rubbish thrown in more loosely; and it was only at a very modern date that houses were built on it.

The outer or "new quay", although of later date than the inner, repairs and restorations excepted, is of considerable age. That it must have been wanted for protection to boats and vessels, is obvious from what we now experience in stormy weather; but the exact date of its erection is not known. It runs nearly at right angles with the old pier and in a direction nearly east and west. Dating from contemporary circumstances, this pier was much injured by a very heavy gale in 1774. As it stood previous to this, it was probably not more than two-thirds of its present length, for the junction of the old and new work is marked by an alteration of form, and in the manner of building. The cost of re-erection was borne by Mr. Long, the then lord of the manors of Rafiel and Lansallos, who actively superintended the work, the fishermen contributing their assistance by bringing the stones from the neighbouring shores and cliffs. On the 20th January, 1817, a storm of unusual violence occurred. Its direction was from the S.E., a very unfavourable point; and the sea, being driven by a furious gale to an extraordinary height, swept away a great deal of property. It covered the "Green" from one end to the other, and reached to the top of the parapet wall of the bridge there, a height of five feet, and stopped the mill-wheel with its violence. The tide, in a body, swept over the highest point of the Peak, and, as near as the eye could judge, at double the height of the rock, not in mere spray, but in a solid body of water. The premises occupied by the Coast-guard were soon levelled with the beach; the shipwrights' yard on Consona rocks, and a cellar and chamber over it, were demolished, with two *stop* and two *tuck* seans there stored. About thirty large boats and a great many smaller were utterly destroyed, so that scarcely a piece could be recognised, the wreck strewing the harbour and streets. Happily no lives were lost, though the danger to many was imminent. The damage done was estimated at upwards of £2,000.

The misfortune to the poor fishermen was exceedingly great, as they were thus deprived of the means of supporting themselves and families. The Sand Quay was rebuilt immediately, and the shipwrights'y ard in the spring; the rebuilding of the Outer Pier was begun on the 16th April following, and this, together with the repair of the Inner Pier, occupied seven months. The height of the former was made about a foot above what it was before.

Behind the quay, and in the side of the hill is a cavern, known as "Willy Willcock's hole", which is believed by the fisher-boys to extend into the bowels of the hill to a distance directly under Landaviddy. They tell you that many years ago, a man, Willy Willcock, essaying the truth of this opinion, crept with difficulty through the narrow opening at the back of the cave, and got entangled in its inner mazes. He was never afterwards seen, but the shrieks of his disturbed ghost are yet plainly to be heard in the hill after night-fall.

In our crescentic sweep of the hauen we pass by another smaller cavern and reach the Peak, with its builder's yard and sail-loft perched on its sheltered side, and ending in a submerged ridge, "The Raney".

Above this last-mentioned cavern is a favourite place of outlook, from which may be had a fine view of the sea. A walk of a hundred yards will discover to you all that expanse of water included between Ramehead and the Deadman: and when the weather is clear, beyond the former may be seen the Bolthead like a thin strip of blue on the horizon. Above this point, in our survey, may be observed the almost obliterated remains of a chapel which have given a name to the whole hill. It was dedicated to St. Peter, the patron saint of Polperro and of fishermen generally. This conspicuous situation was probably chosen, that whilst it might serve as a landmark, mariners might also direct their vows to it when in distress. The chapel of St. Peter de Porthpyre, (Polperro), is mentioned in 1392, and this is the earliest, and indeed only written evidence I can find of its existence.

We suffer greatly from south-westerly gales, but the winds which affect us most are those blowing from points between south and east. We have records of gales from the latter direction, some of which have been already mentioned, which have threatened to demolish the town. In the time of a storm Polperro is a striking scene of bustle and excitement. The noise of the wind as it roars up the coomb, the hoarse rumbling of the angry sea, the shouts of the fishermen engaged in securing their boats, and the screams of the women and children, carrying the tidings of the latest disaster, are a peculiarly melancholy assemblage of sounds, especially

POLPERRO. By F. Varty.

After Wm. Daniell 1825.

14

when heard at midnight. All who can render assistance are out of their beds, helping the sailors and fishermen; lifting the boats out of reach of the sea, or taking the furniture of the ground floors to a place of safety. The excitement is extreme, but not more than is necessary to the occasion, for with the loss of his boat the fisherman is deprived of the most important of his possessions, as well as of his means of obtaining a livelihood. When the first streak of morning light comes, bringing no cessation of the storm, but only serving to show the devastation it has made, the effect is still more dismal. The wild fury of the waves is a sight of no mean grandeur as it dashes over the peak, and falls on its jagged summit, from whence it streams down its sides in a thousand waterfalls, and foams at its base. The infuriated sea sweeps over the piers, and striking against the rocks and houses on the warren side, rebounds towards the strand, and washes fragments of houses and boats into the streets where the receding tide leaves them strewn in sad confusion. Storms of this kind I have seen several times, though happily they are not of very frequent occurrence.

The houses are almost all of modern date, and none are of any considerable age; the most ancient being probably those on the southern side of Lansallos-street, to which the ugly gables, projecting into the road, are more recent additions. One house in the row, indeed, has marks of antiquity, especially in its curiously constructed roof. Those nearest the river in the same street are built nearly after one fashion, and that a strange and inconvenient one, with low roofs, doors which require you to stoop very low on entering, and a ground floor below the level of the street. The date marked on the ceiling of one shows that it was in being in the reign of James II. In many of these the lower floor is put to the purpose of a fish-cellar, the second floor or dwelling room being reached by a flight of steps terminating in a porch, locally called an "orrel". The dwelling room is usually clean, and well sprinkled with sand from *Leak-rock*, roofed by the unplastered floors and beams of the sleeping apartments above, and garnished with china from over the sea. To a beam may be noticed affixed the *nessel-taker*, a rude but ingenious device for the home production of the *nessel* or snood to which the hook is immediately attached.

From what I have been able to trace, and learn from tradition, the houses must have multiplied to twice their number within little more than one hundred years; and it is certain that their conveniences and appearance have been much improved. Throughout the whole of the cliff, from the East to the Lower Bridge, there was no house on the seaward site of the present street. The best houses in Talland are modern, not only in erection, but on new ground. The houses from Cove-head to "Old Quay" are of late date; and within the memory of people I have known, there was only one Green, and that a play-ground, for the village boys. There was much contention and ill-will connected with the building of the houses that separate the Little and Great Greens, as they are now called. In fact, the building of the larger houses, was an encroachment on public rights; and since then, the existence of any garden before a house in the Little Green, however small, is not less an encroachment.

15

The streets are narrow, tortuous, and badly paved, but picturesque from their very want of plan. There were formerly many thatched roofs, but the last was torn down during the past century. The houses are built with the utmost disregard of perpendicular and horizontal lines in their proportions, and of what we now consider ordinary convenience in their internal arrangement; yet they cannot be called huts even for the sake of heightening a description. On the Talland side the buildings reach on each side of the old road as high as half way up the rugged hill to a place named in a spirit of pleasantry, one would suppose, "Head o' ditch", but sometimes more poetically called "Sun rising". They also reach in the opposite direction through the coomb to "Fishing bridge".

A few words about our roads will suffice in this brief description. The road through the coomb on the Talland side of the stream leads to Crumplehorn, where four ways divaricate; one by Langreek, Lansallos, and Fowey; another up the hill by Killiow to Lerrin and Lostwithiel; a smaller path takes you through Long-coomb valley to Pelynt; and lastly, the most considerable, or *new road*, which winds round the hills of Pleaton and Killigarth. This new road was cut in 1849, and is so important to the traffic of the town, that the stranger who misses his way, and descends on horseback the old Talland road, if he has time to spare on any subject than the safety of himself and horse, will be puzzled to conceive how we contrived to do so long without it. It is one of the greatest improvements which the town has seen within living memory. Another road leads out of the town westward by Landaviddy and Rafiel to join the road to Lansallos by Crumplehorn and Langreek. It is curious that weddings and funerals invariably proceed by this way to the church of Lansallos, though it is by no means the shortest.

There any many views in the ground thus mapped, which are re-markable for their romantic beauty. The prospect from the top of Brent is fine in a high degree. You are immediately impressed with the *unusual* character of the scene, and the remarkable absence of the conventional in its outline and details. In a storm it must be terribly grand, but who can fancy himself on that bleak eminence in a storm? On a fine summer's day it will give you ample satisfaction for the toil of the ascent. The summit of the hill on which you stand is broken by pointed crags, which give a bold and appropriate character to the foreground, while outspread before you is the broad blue sea dotted with ships, and defined on the left by the Ramehead and the more distant headlands; while on the right the Deadman, and if clear, the Lizard Points, bound the view. Immediately below are the harbour, valley, and town of Polperro; the Peak, with its striking jagged outline and massive black colouring; the sail-loft resting in a recess on its side; the ledges of rocks, here and there hollowed into caverns, and the quays, between which are the fishing boats riding quietly in tiers. Further up among the hills which shut this scene in, you see strange, and apparently confused, groups of houses, having a general tint of whitewash, and above them, on the southern side, the little chapel of St. John. The hills which overtop this scene are, on the south, and south-west, *Kayne*, and the taller *Hard-head*, the former with its most irregular spine of rock and wall running along its summit,

16

and dotted on its seaward side by miniature houses built for the drying of fish. Landward of the town rises Hobb's hill, here seen in profile, with the houses on its base and sides. The curve of the coomb prevents you from including more than a third of the town. In the sweep of the hill to the west may be noticed Landaviddy peeping from a clump of sycamore. Other views of the same character, but having much of variety, may be had from Kayne, and the little farm opposite Jowter's park.

The sea-coast is of a very interesting character, and will repay the visit of the man of science, as well as the more superficial tourist. It is formed by tall and stately hills, rising abruptly out of the sea, to the height of three of four hundred feet, and having their sides roughened by craggy rocks. They are chiefly appropriated to the feeding of sheep, and are covered in some places with considerable patches of furze. When culti- vated they carry good crops of turnips and wheat. At their bases are precipitous cliffs, looking like a series of semi-circular excavations; to which the erosion of the sea and the frosts and thaws of winter are con- stantly making additions. The whole ends in a margin of rock, consisting of ledges of blue, brey, and red slate, interstratified by lines of trap, which run along in the course of the stratification, following it in all its sinuosities. The land retires on the eastern side of Polperro to form Talland bay; and a little to the west is another indentation called Lan- tivet bay.

Acknowledgments . . .

We wish to thank Chapman and Hall for permission to reproduce the drawings of Polperro (page 60) and Talland Church (page 27) from their book the "*Cornish Coast*. The drawing on page 36 is from "*The Smugglers*" by Charles Harper, also published by Chapman and Hall.

17

2

LANSALLOS

It is a pleasant, though perhaps an unprofitable employment to speculate on what may have been the ancient condition of a place, concerning which, few or no memorials of any antiquity are found to exist. Yet he must have a very laggard fancy who has not found himself attempting to pierce the mists, however dark, which hang over the history of the spot on which his life has been passed; peopling the familiar hills and vales with the men of former times, and entering into their habits and usages as dimly shadowed forth by the fragments which time has left to him. I shall, however, here only deal with simple facts, although I may be permitted to think that the little fishing-town of Polperro, though it has no records of past, or pretensions to present importance, may have had an existence as an inhabited place at a time anterior to the date of many of those larger towns, whose magnificent ports give shelter to the ships, which are at once the glory and safeguard of Britain. Our British forefathers probably found these small, but commodious creeks, best adapted to their rude skiffs. But we have something more than conjecture to show that this place was a considerable village, in Saxon and Norman times. In those days the thane or lord resided in his castle or other house, having inherent sovereignty over his domain and its peasantry, whilst in the neighbourhood was the *village* where dwelt that portion of the community then known as *ceorls* or *villains* engaged in the necessary husbandry and other occupations, law-worthy, but in a condition which rendered them almost a portion of the soil they tilled. Now within a small circuit of Polperro we have the separate manors of Killigarth, Talland, and Trelawne on the one hand, and of Rafiel and Lansallos on the other, the ceorls appertaining to which had a chief residence in this village. As an existing proof of this, take the following facts. On the Talland side of the town is a triangular piece of land, cut out, as it were, from the manor of Killigarth, its base drawn from "Higher Shute" towards the sea, to meet the road leading to the warren; and its sides marked by the paths which start from each of those points to meet the apex at a spot where now stands the Wesleyan Association Chapel. Within this triangle a portion of the village was contained, for it is parcelled out into several portions, which to this day belong to the several manors mentioned above, being held of the lord of Killigarth by payment of a nominal fee, except portions which have been lately transferred by sale. The strip nearest the base of the triangle was sold by Carpenter, the owner of Rafiel, on the partition of that estate; the contiguous part is the property of General Buller, the proprietor of Killiow and of other estates in the vicinity. Then follow strips belonging to Trelawny of Trelawne, Kendall of Killigarth, and Morth Woolcombe of Talland. This triangular spot did not contain the whole of Polperro, as Rafiel and Killigarth had the remainder of the space which Polperro now occupies.

"Our forefathers in the village", to quote the words of Gilbert White, "were no doubt as busy and bustling and as important as ourselves; yet have their names and transactions been forgotten from century to century", and little record remains even to tell of the existence of Polperro at an early date.

I shall now make a survey of the western parish which shares Polperro with Talland, on the east.

Lansallos is in the Hundred and Deanery of West, and is included for electoral purposes, in the Eastern Division of the County of Cornwall; in the Petty Sessional Division of Trecan Gate; in the County-court jurisdiction of Liskeard, and the Liskeard Poor-Law Union. It is bordered on the east by Talland, on the north by Pelynt, and on the north-west by Lanreath. St. Veep slightly impinges on it a little further west, while Lanteglos, (juxta Fowey) forms its western boundary, and the English Channel washes its southern side.

The titheable lands amount to 2,700 acres of which 2,506 are arable; 70 acres meadow and pasture; 11 acres woodland; 33 acres orchard and garden; and 80 acres rough pasturage. The living is a rectory in the patronage of Francis Howell, Esq., and the tithes were commuted in 1840 at £500 per annum.

On our way by Landaviddy to the Church-town we pass by Saint's Well, a perennial spring associated now with the patronage of no particular saint, but having the fame of special virtues. Its reputation has long survived the entire destruction of the edifice which surrounded it; for it is still resorted to by those afflicted with bad eyes and other ailments, and, if "ceremonies due are done aright", with great benefit. It must be visited on three mornings following before sunrise, fasting; a relic of a veritable ceremony, as witnesseth Chaucer's Pardoner:—

> "If that the goode man that the beest oweth
> Wol every wike, er that the cok him croweth,
> Fastynge, drynke of this well a draught,
> As thilke holy Jew our eldres taught,
> His beestes and his stoor schal multiplie."

We next halt at Rafiel. This manor appears to be the one mentioned in the Domesday Survey under the name of Raswale, when it was the property of the Earl of Moreton.

The manor of Lansallos is further west, and nearer the Church-town. In the Domesday book it is called Lansalhus; in the Exeter Domesday Lansalous, and it is mentioned in the former as being held under the Earl Moreton.

Lansallos, as its name implies, and so many circumstances denote, was once a place of no ordinary sanctity. That it was far back a place of refuge, possessing peculiar privileges, is evident from the number of roads that converge to it from all directions, a number strangely out of proportion to the present low importance of the place. The one leading from the beach to the Churchtown is even paved. There is, moreover, a field close to the church called Sentry or Sanctuary to this day.

The church is a venerable structure, consisting of a chancel, nave, and north and south aisles; the south separated by an arcade of six four-centred arches, and the north by three of similar construction. The mouldings of the pillars are buried in numerous layers of white-wash. The pulpit and singing gallery in the nave are of very modern date, and built in the very worst taste. The finely carved bench-ends are decayed and patched, and in many places they have been removed and replaced by high-backed pews of plain deal. The little carving that remains, both on seat and roof, is of a very good character. The windows are of the very plainest kind, the thick granite mullions running straight up to the arch, without tracery or slightest foliation above. The tower arch spring from corbels of sculptured foliage. The church, indeed, has been so patched and altered that little of any interest remains.

On our way back to Polperro, we shall see at a little distance, the farm of Killiow, once the seat of a family of that name, extinct in 1711.

A little above Crumplehorn, which we soon reach, are the scant remains of a small but ancient and rude house, concerning which I will here insert a story which I first heard from my mother, but is still told by the country people near. Judging from my mother's age and remembrance, the tale must be at least a hundred and fifty years old.

There is a place up the Coomb known as "Old Walls", from obscure marks of buildings. The situation is extraordinary, because there is no road leading to it; the brook is immediately in front; and around, for two-thirds of the site, is marshy ground. Yet there are even now on the hill-side of the house some garden flowers, and others which were cultivated for medicinal purposes; the pretty blue periwinkle (*Vinca minor*), the daffodil, the green hellebore (*Helleborus viridis*), and others, still maintaining a struggle with the wild weeds of neglect. These old walls once harboured two maiden sisters, unknown in their other relationship, and uncared for by any. They were harmless, meddled with none, and even shunned their kind; so they lived unmolested, until one or two sheep were missed by a neighbouring farmer, when suspicion fell on them, through the difficulty of accounting for their means of support. They did not appear to labour, and were, indeed, incapable of it. By authority of a warrant, their house was searched, and nothing was found but a quantity of snails salted in pots for their food. It is to be wished that the names and history of these honest people had been preserved; but those who had lived on under much distress, and who had retired to this solitary place for shelter from the world's neglect, could not survive the suspicion of guilt, and died soon after. The remains of their dwelling are still associated with the remembrance of their story.

3

TALLAND

Crossing the brook at Polperro into Talland, we may find enough to interest us in a walk through so much of it as lies in the neighbourhood.

On the top of the eastern hill, and a little to the left of the road which leads to the church, is the neat old manor-house of Killigarth, with its antique square-headed and granite-mullioned windows, its respectable arched door-ways, and massive chimneys. On a stone in front of the house are Greek and Latin inscriptions, which translated read as follows:—

"All things, (or these things), are to the glory of God". "Freely ye have received, freely give". "God will bring these things also to an end". The second sentence is a quotation, from the Greek New Testament; and the third is from the Æneid, being part of an address made by Æneas to his fellow Trojan wanderers. I suppose the stone must have formerly belonged to some building erected for a charitable purpose; and, from the appearance of the letters, their date can be hardly set down as anterior to the Reformation, if so ancient.

The house has on the second stage, a fine room, now used as a sleeping apartment; but, from its dimensions and the labour bestowed on its decoration, evidently once the state room of the house. Its ceiling is vaulted, and divided by longitudinal and transverse mouldings; each compartment containing some event in the history of Paradise, illustrated by grotesque figures of its winged and four-footed inhabitants. Outside the house, a double hedge, of great width, runs by the side of the road, and is still in good preservation, though not, as once, perhaps, adorned by topiary art, and used as a place of promenade.

Killigarth was probably the property of John de Kylgat, who is mentioned by Carew as one of those having estates of £20 per annum in the time of Edward I. In the reign of Henry VI, it became the property of the Beres, by whom it was transmitted by an heiress to the Bevilles. Sir William, of that name, resided here in Queen Elizabeth's time, and later, when the old house was "much visited through his frank invitings". Carew says "Killigarth being interpreted in English, signifieth he hath lost his griping, or reaching; and by his present fortune, (in some sort), justifieth that name; for the same hath lately foregone Sir William Beville, whom it embraced as owner and inhabitant, by his sudden death; and is passed into the possession of the fair lady, his widow, by her husband's conveyance". The good Knight was the last male heir of an ancient and respectable family. Tradition states that after long and faithful service of his sovereign, he returned to Killigarth, where he kept an hospitable house, and lived honoured by his dependants; until one day, as he was walking through his fields, he was attacked by a furious bull, and gored to death. The story may have some truth in it, but I suspect it to have been suggested since his time, by the frequent occurrence of the bull in the heraldic devices on his tomb in Talland Church. The arms of the family were: *Argent, a bull passant gules, armed and tipped or.*

"The mention of this Knight", says Carew, *"calleth to my remembrance a sometimes uncouth servant of his, whose monstrous conditions partly resembled that Polyphemus, described by Homer and Virgil, and lively imitated by Ariosto in his Orco; or rather that Egyptian Polyphagus in whome, (by Suetonius' report), the Emperor Nero took such pleasure. This fellow was taken up by Sir William under a hedge in the deepest of winter, well neere starved with cold and hunger. He was of stature meane, of constitution leane; of face freckled, of composition well-proportioned, of diet, naturally spare and cleanly enough; yet at his master's bidding he would devoure nettles, thistles, the pith of artichokes, raw, and living birds and fishes, with their scales and feathers, burning coles and candles, and whatsoever else, however unsavorie, if it might be swallowed. Neither this a little, but in such quantitie as it often bred a second wonder how his belly could contain so much. Yet could no man at any time discover him doing of that which necessitie of Nature requireth. Moreover he would take a hot yron out of the fire with his bare hand; never changed his apparell but by constraint; and used to lie in strawe with his heade downe and his heels upwards. Spare he was of speech, and insteade of halfe his words used this term, size; as 'I will size him', for 'strike him'. 'Hee is a good size' for man, &c. Over sleeping, or some other accident, made him to lose a day in his account of the weeke, so as he would not beleeve but that Sunday was Saterday, Saterday Friday, &c. To Sir William he bare such faithfulnesse that he would follow his horse like a spanyell without regard of way or wearinesse, waite at his chamber doore the night time, suffering none to come neere him, and performe whatsoever he commanded, were it never so unlawful or dangerous. On a time, his master expecting strangers, sent him with a panier to his cater at the sea-side, to fetch some fish. In his way he passed by a river whereinto the tide then flowed, and certaine fisherman were drawing their nets; which after John Size had awhile beheld, he casts to have a share amongst them, for his master. So into the water he leaps, and then, for the space of a flight shoot, wadeth and walloweth, (for swim he could not), sometimes up and sometimes down, carrying his pannier still before him to his own extreme hazard of drowning, and the beholders' great pittying, until at last all wet and wearied, out he scrambleth, and home he hieth with a bitter complaint to his master of his ill-fortune that hee could not catch some fish as well as the rest where so much were going. In this sort he continued for divers yeeres, until (upon I know not what veake or unkindness), away he gets, and abroad he rogues, which remitter brought him in the end to his fore-deffered and not avoyded destiny; for as under a hedge hee was found pyning, so under a hedge he found his miserable death through penury."*

Leaving Killigarth we make the steep descent of Sandhill, where in the memory of very old men, was a furze-brake from whence Polperro obtained a considerable part of its fuel before coal was extensively used. Talland beach is at the foot of the hill, and is crossed in our way to the church. Here the sea is fretting the land considerably, nearly half the meadow seaward of the road having disappeared within the last fifty years. At the bottom of the hill on which the church is situated is "Rotterdam", where there was within remembrance a mill, connected with the exploit of a Breton miller, soon to be given in full.

In the County histories, when treating of this parish, the name is derived from *tal* and *lan* and supposed to mean the high church; but this explanation is very unsatisfactory, as the situation of the church is on a lower level than any of its neighbours, and the general elevation of the land around is not such as to give it this implied pre-eminence. It would rather seeem that the designation of the parish is no older than the date of the church, and is obtained from the Saint to whom it is dedicated. The *Monasticon Exoniensis*, while it gives no date, informs us that the patron was S. Tallanus. It is difficult now to discover by what circumstance the choice of a tutelary saint was governed, but it is still more difficult to suppose that this choice was arbitrary or fanciful. The name of the parish may have been intended to perpetuate the fame of some holy man whose sanctity was the glory of the spot, or perhaps of the day in which the edifice was reared. All records of S. Tallanus are lost to us.

The church is a plain but picturesque structure, consisting of two aisles separated by granite pillars like those of Lansallos church. The northern aisle projects at the eastern end to form the chancel, and in its gable is a window of three lancet lights with slight foliations. Leading into this aisle is a short north transept in which are the seats of the Killigarth house.

During repairs it was found necessary to take down a portion of the north wall; and the removal of the whitewash discovered a number of frescoes which would have been destroyed without leaving even a memorial of their existence, had not my friend, Dr. Box, been accidentally on the spot. "These frescoes", he says, "consisted of two series laid one on the other; the first, (that nearest to the wall), was executed in colours, while the other was traced in black, and, being on a white ground, its figures were displayed in bold relief. Both, unfortunately, were much defaced by exposure to heavy rains, and in attempting to separate them, many portions of each were unavoidably destroyed. Among the subjects of the original, or coloured series, (some parts of which were comparatively perfect), was an imposing representation of the crucifixion. The body of the Saviour was well-proportioned, and the contortions displayed by the muscles of its upper portion showed great suffering. The countenance possessed a Grecian cast: it was oval, with regular features, and bore a mingled expression of pain and resignation. On the head was placed a large crown of gilded thorns, and from a wound in the left side issued, in rapid succession, large drops of blood, which formed a continuous line to the ground. The most remarkable feature in this picture was the unaccountable vividness of colour displayed by the blood. It has been said by an able connoisseur of frescoes that 'we may as well expect to find in them great softness and delicacy of finish, as richness or *depth of colour*, for that they are equally impossible; in this instance, however, such was the striking effect produced by the peculiar intensity and brilliancy of the colour, that it was doubted whether the richest oil paintings of any age ever equalled it.

Standing at a short distance on the right of the cross were two female figures, enveloped in dark-coloured drapery, and at the foot stood a fine specimen of a Roman soldier, gazing apparently with great interest at the sufferer.

Another drawing represented the short figure of a person clad in a loose dark overcoat or cloak, which reached a little below the knees, standing by a well, or rather, what appeared to be three wells or fountains, which were surrounded by a small circular stone wall, and who, by means of an apparatus erected above the centre one, was drawing water in a primitive-looking bucket, while a man in a rude costume, was departing from the well with an utensil, made apparently of skin or leather, suspended to his back by means of a hunting spear that rested on his left shoulder.

The next, and most perfect, of these pictures, was that of a large ship under sail, which, from her slanting position on the surface of the water, appeared to be mounting over a long swell of the sea. The vessel had four masts; on the two foremost, large sails were set, while the others were furnished, after the Greek fashion, with lateen-shaped sails; her sides were decorated with six gaily painted bands or streaks, which were separately charged with saltires and crosses of opposite colours, such as a red band with a black cross, a green with a red saltire, &c., and each mast-head was ornamented with a square green flag bearing a red saltire, which is commonly known as the cross of St. Andrew.

Besides these drawings many fragments and detached portions of various figures were scattered over the wall, which were equally curious and attractive in themselves, but too numerous and minute to admit of a separate description. There was a curious group of detached members of a human figure near to the ship, however, which deserves a short notice. The small space that it occupied, and the positions in which the objects were placed, clearly showed that they could not have been intended to represent a perfect living figure. This group was rendered conspicuous by the bold outlines and striking effect produced by an isolated right hand and arm, which were intermixed with several smaller objects of less interest. The hand was horizontally placed, with the first and second fingers extended towards the west, in the direction of the picture of the crucifixion; while the third and fourth were closed upon the palm. The arm, which was dismembered at the shoulder and the wrist, was also in a horizontal position, and flexed at the elbow with the fore-arm pointed downwards.

These coloured frescoes were supposed to be as old as the church itself, being only separated from the wall by a thin layer of plaster. On these was subsequently laid another coat of plaster to receive the next series, consisting of the most horrible and fantastic images, traced in black.

One of the most prominent amongst these was a picture of the devil, which, possessing apparently, as much of the horrible as human ingenuity could possibly devise, might with justice have been considered by the most critical observer among those for whom it was intended as at least a respectable likeness. He was represented in an erect posture, with a dark mantle thrown over his shoulders, and fastened at the neck; with his hands, or hairy paws, clasped together by claws instead of fingers, uplifted and rested on the breast in a supplicating attitude; his head was adorned with two thick black horns, bent a little backwards; and the balls of his enormous round eyes were painted a brilliant red, to which an additional horror was imparted by their being surrounded with a slight circle of white. The lower part of his person was not clearly seen. At the foot of this figure was a large hindmost limb, (disgustingly plain), of some loathsome monster that was dimly seen beneath the whitewash, trailing along the ground with its claws stuck into the soil to aid progression apparently in the act of retreating towards the west. On the left, and about the centre of the wall, a nun was figured, sitting in a pensive attitude; her cheek rested on the back of a hideous dwarf. The only remaining object clearly defined was a house which appeared on the eastern extremity of the wall. It had two curious small square windows, divided into a number of apertures, apparently by strong bars of wood crossing each other at right angles. The door was also of small dimensions, and secured on the outside by large bolts, which gave it the true character of a prison.

"By now standing", says Dr. Box, "at a short distance, so as to command a comprehensive view of the wall, such an incongruous tableau of parti-coloured objects and figures was here displayed as cannot be easily imagined. In immediate contact with the Saviour on the Cross, attended by a group of mourning females and Roman soldiers in various coloured costumes, was seen the devil surrounded by imps and monsters, all in black; a sorrowful nun, accompanied by an ugly grinning dwarf, close to a party of lively figures engaged in pastoral pursuits; a beautifully decorated ship under sail, as if about to force an entrance into the dark interior of a frowning prison, &c. The effect of the scene was equally novel and absurd".

The tower is remarkable being built on a hillock above and apart fom the church on its south and west side, and connected with it by a low porch only. It is a plain battlemented structure devoid of ornament, and built of the slate stones of the neighbourhood, a portion having been brought from the beach below, as appears from the shells of serpulae and other calcareous animals still visible on their exposed surfaces. Of the date of the church and tower nothing certain is known.

The old vicarage house, which was near the church, has been recently pulled down. It was a curious old-fashioned building with a curtilage in front, entered by a low doorway in the wall.

Somewhat more than a century back the vicarage was held by the Rev. Richard Dodge, a strange and eccentric character, whose fame is not yet extinct among us. He was supposed to have some knowledge of magic, and to be an especially powerful exorcist. His prayer was dreaded by spirits of air, earth, or other place. Refractory ghosts who had withstood the combined power of seven priests in league against them, have fled at his single word. The fisherman feloniously cutting willows about midnight for the manufacture of his crabpots, has been frightened from his dishonest work by the loud sound of Parson Dodge's whip, and presently after by a troop of turbulent spirits gliding down 'Bridle Lane' towards the sea, in which they were laid. "He was", says Bond, "a very worthy man, and much respected, but had his eccentricities". His tombstone may still be seen in the higher churchyard, though in fragments, and the following inscription made out:—

Here lieth the body of the Rev. Mr. Richard Dodge, late of Talland, vicar, who departed this life the 13th day of January, 1746, in the 93rd year of his age.

Since then the old vicarage house had had another notable tenant, whose story has not become legendary, since the circumstances occurred so lately as the year 1812, and are therefore fresh in the memories of persons still living, from whom, and my own recollection, I gather the following facts.

About the time mentioned, the Rev. Mr. Whitmore, a gentleman of polished habits and prepossessing appearance, came to Talland, and, after a while, made the acquaintance of the Vicar. He represented himself as having recently been the incumbent of a living in Ireland, but that, having just come into the enjoyment of a liberal fortune, he preferred to enjoy it in some retired corner of England. Professing to be mightily taken with the seclusion of Talland, his offer to serve it as curate was accepted by the vicar, who held also the living of Lanlivery. He soon settled himself in the vicarage-house, and fitted it up in a style which its rude low rooms had probably never before known. He kept a good table, was very hearty in his invitations, and his neighbours showed a full appreciation of his hospitality. He was a very pleasant companion, and had many social accomplishments, though, withal, a little too convivial in his habits. To the poor of his parish he was affable and kind. The duties of the church were conducted with great order and solemnity. I cannot discover by what means he contrived to get the Bishop's licence, but certain it is that he was so far recognised as to be selected to read prayers or preach before the Archdeacon at one of his visitations. Though his munificence and general behaviour for a long time disarmed doubt, there was at length some inkling of the imposture. The suspicion spread, as it always does, whether well or ill-founded; his drafts were dishonoured at Job's bank, and he was soon beseiged by uneasy creditors. Immediately, and with great privacy, he packed up such plate and valuables as could be easily carried about his person, all, or most of which, were unpaid for, and decamped, leaving folks to wonder as much at their own stupidity as his craft. His subsequent history is not traced, except the end of it. With the hardihood which characterised his general career, he visited Bristol, where, before his visit to Talland, he had committed serious forgeries. Here Robert Peacock, (his real name is doubtful), was recognised beneath his disguise, apprehended, and convicted of his crimes. A person of Polperro, who had often heard him in Talland church, happened to be passing through Gloucester at the time, and witnessed his death on the gallows. He had of course married several couples during his curacy, who were thrown into consternation at the thought that their marriage bond was invalid. There must have been great laxity somewhere, or such an imposture could not have been allowed; but we cannot fail to be astonished at the daring of a man who could cover his frauds with the sacred vestments of the Church, and thus recklessly scandalize the holy calling of a minister of the Gospel.

TALLAND CHURCH.

Carew has fortunately preserved a story about Talland manor house; for tradition has only kept unconnected fragments. The most probable date of the circumstance is the time of the French War which immediately followed the accession of Henry VIII., and the person so abducted was the John Murth, who married Joan, daughter and heiress of John Talland.

"One of their auncestors, within the memorie of a next neighbour to the house, called Prake, *(burdened with* 110 *yeeres age), entertained a British (Breton) miller, as that people for such idle occupations proue more handie than our owne. But this fellowes seruice befell commodious in the worst sense. For when, not long after his acceptance, warres grewe betweene vs and France, he stealeth ouer into his countrey, returneth priuily backe againe, with a French crew, surprizeth suddenly his master and his ghests at a Christmas supper, carrieth them speedily into Lantreghey, and forceth the Gent. to redeeme his enlargement with the sale of a great part of his reuenewes".*

Mr. Bond remembered seeing in the old house, a part of which was a few years since torn down, "a secret doorway behind a chest of

27

drawers, which was said to have been placed there to prevent another mishap of the above, or similar kind".

Adjoining the Talland estate on the north-west is Portallow, probably the manor mentioned in Domesday as Portatlant, which may one have included Talland, but it is now separated, and the property of Trelawny.

4

SMUGGLING AND PRIVATEERING

"The race of yore
Who danced our infancy upon their knee,
And told our marvelling boyhood, legends store
Of strange adventures happ'd by land or sea:
How are they blotted from the things that be!"

Our town was probably a stronghold of the contraband trade in early times, and my description would be incomplete without some mention of it. The place was especially adapted to its successful prosecution. A commodious creek led into a deep and secluded valley, of very difficult approach by land; where lived a race of hardy and reckless sailors, and amphibious artizans, for whom a life of adventure, and great, though precarious, profits had many charms. All joined in it; the smith left his forge, and the husbandman his plough; even women and children turned out to assist in the unlawful traffic, and received their share of the proceeds. That it was in any degree a dishonest pursuit perhaps never entered their minds; and if it did, they was enough in the conduct of those above them to satisfy less unscrupulous minds that theirs was a venial offence. The gentry of the neighbourhood bought their brandy and lace; the excise and custom-house officers connived at unlawful acts, and profited by secret connection with the smugglers. Revenue cruisers were not unfrequently detected with contraband goods on board, and sometimes caught in the fact. As there is a strong natural propensity to the hunting and snaring of wild beasts, which the most stringent forest and game laws are unable to repress, so there seems to have be an instinctive disposition to smuggling, which will show itself even when the gains bear no proportion to the risk. And it must be confessed, when listening to the sailor's recitals of his deeds in this line, admiration of his skill and daring leads up to forget that they were not such as sober judgment could commend.

The ships employed were first built elsewhere; but, with the increase of money, it was found more convenient to build them at home, and accordingly yards were erected on Consona Rocks and the Peak. Fine craft, too, they turned out—clippers, which, when manned by skilful and intrepid sailors, would scud away from the fastest of the Government cruisers, and offer them a tow-rope in derision. One vessel, the *Unity*, is stated to have made five hundred successful trips, and to have served on some privateering expeditions, without having met with a single serious misadventure. In these vessels were perpetrated so many overt acts of defiance against law, and so much contempt of authority was shewn, as to lead one to doubt that the circumstances could have occurred within so recent a date.

The following incidents are derived from oral testimony, and will give an idea of the open and daring manner in which the trade was carried on at Polperro, towards the end of the last and beginning of the present century.

On one occasion intelligence had been received at Fowey, that a "run of goods" had been effected at Polperro during the previous night, and several men of a cutter's crew were accordingly sent as scouts to get all the information they could as to where the cargo was secreted. At Landaviddy they met with a farm labourer, who had, it was suspected, been engaged in many transactions of this sort, and in this one in particular. They tried to extract information from him by stratagem; but, finding that he was not to be entrapped, they tried the opposite plan, and threatened him with immediate impressment into the King's service if he did not tell them where the goods were hidden. They succeeded in frightening him, and he informed them that a large number of kegs were stowed in a certain cellar above Yellow-rock, and he promised to go and distinguish the place by a chalk-mark on the door. Having, from the opposite hill, seen this done, a portion of the crew returned to Fowey to get an augmentation of their force. Headed by the Custom-house officers, they soon returned, and proceeded in the direction of the cellar. The arrival of the force and their object were discovered, and a band of desperate smugglers, armed with cutlasses and pistols, assembled on New Quay Head, which place commanded an open view of the cellar that contained the kegs. A large gun was drawn down, loaded and pointed, while a man with a match stood by, waiting the command of the skipper to fire. The revenue men were then defied and threatened in a loud and determined tone. They consulted their prudence, and resolved to send for a still stronger force. In a few hours a well-armed band arrived, and rushed into the cellar, but found, to their great disappointment, that, although the place had been watched from the outside, the kegs which had really been there, had been removed they knew not whither.

Happily their resistance rarely led to bloodshed, and in those instances where life was lost, it was generally on the side of the "free-traders".

In the month of December, 1802, as the day was drawing to a close, a Revenue cruiser was seen in pursuit of the *Vigilant*, the latter making all haste with a strong south-west breeze to enter the harbour, into which they felt sure their pursuers would not follow them. Night came on before the harbour was gained, but this was to the advantage of the smugglers, who well knew how to enter even in the deepest darkness. No chance of a capture therefore remained to the cruiser except by cutting away the gear of the smack by shot, and thereby compelling her to heave to. A running fire was kept up with considerable effect; but the vessel was not so far disabled but that she ran into the harbour and landed her kegs in safety. Two men, however, lost their lives in the *Vigilant*.

The last affair in which life was lost was in 1810, when Robert Mark was shot. He lies in Talland churchyard with the following lines for his epitaph:—

"The Revenue men were then defied . . ."

> *"In prime of life most suddenly,*
> *Sad tidings to relate,*
> *(Here view my utter destiny*
> *And pity my sad fate,)*
> *I, by a shot which rapid flew*
> *Was instantly struck dead.*
> *Lord! pardon the offender who*
> *My precious blood did shed.*
> *Grant him to rest and forgive me*
> *All I have done amiss;*
> *And that I may rewarded be*
> *With everlasting bliss".*

The story of Tom Potter, which I shall next relate, created considerable feeling at the time, and is still told with expressions of pity for his fate. One morning, I forget in what year, a lugger was descried by the crew of a revenue boat, then stationed on shore. She was lying quietly becalmed in Whitsand Bay. The glass informed them that it was the *Lottery*, of Polperro, well known for her fast sailing qualities, as well as for the hardihood of her crew. There was little doubt that with the springing up of the breeze she would put to sea, and there would be another opportunity of taunt and sneer at the supineness of the revenue forces. Accordingly the officer in command, with all despatch, manned two or three boats and put off, making sure of a rare capture, for there seemed little chance of an escape. Their movements were, however, observed by the smugglers, who made preparation for resistance. The boats, on seeing their intentions, commenced firing when at a considerable distance; but it was not until they had approached her pretty near, that the shots were returned from the lugger, which now assumed an unmistakeable attitude of defiance. When within a few yards of the expected prize, Ambrose Bowden, who pulled the bow-oar of one of the attacking boats, fell mortally wounded. It was plain that the Polperro men had come to a determination not to give up their fine craft and valuable cargo without a struggle, so the boats deemed it their wisest course to withdraw and allow the *Lottery* to proceed to sea. This affray was of course reported to the authorities, and it was determined to mark this daring act of resistance to the law, aggravated by manslaughter, with their highest displeasure. Orders were issued to arrest the vessel, and all or part of her crew, wherever they might be found. The smugglers were alarmed at their act, and from the dogged manner in which the officers of justice pursued them, they saw but little chance of escape. They were kept continually in terror, and were afraid to sleep in their own houses without a watch, or to visit their families except with the utmost secrecy of movement. At the dead of night, or at mid-day they were liable to have their houses surrounded by a troop of dragoons, who made stealthy descents upon the town. They were hidden for days in secret closets, (of which each house had one or more), or wandered the country by night, and lay concealed during the day in the farmers' straw houses, where often the tramp of their pursuers was heard as they passed near their place of concealment.

32

At length one of the crew of the *Lottery*, tired of this hide-and-seek life, and even, perhaps, thinking that his services in so important a matter would be highly rewarded, gave himself up as evidence, and pointed out Tom Potter, one of his comrades, as the man who had fired the shot.

The Polperro people made common cause of it, and their thoughts were divided between a care to preserve Potter from the law, and a feeling of utter detestation of the conduct of Toms, the informer. Their wits were therefore set to work to accomplish the concealment and ultimate escape of the former, and to remove the latter, and with him the only decisive evidence in the case. The revenue men well knew the danger in which Toms stood, and took him into the crew of a cutter which cruised on the coast. On a certain occasion this cutter lay at Polruan, five or six miles westward from Polperro. By the aid of alternate entreaty and threat, and with a solemn promise that no bodily harm should be done to her husband, Toms' wife was persuaded to go to Polruan, (pretending that her visit was a clandestine one), and if, as it was expected would happen, he offered to see her a mile out of town, to accept of his companionship. The event answered the hopes entertained. In the dusk of the evening he was seen leading his wife across the Lantick Downs, when three of four men sprung from behind a hedge, secured him, and carried him off to some place of concealment. So carefully was this managed, that, notwithstanding the most diligent search, he was not to be traced. We are hardly disposed to credit sufficiently the smugglers for their good faith, but it is certain that, though the life of a relative or comrade was concerned in this matter, they kept their word with the wife, and even treated Toms with consideration. They removed him from place to place of concealment as circumstances rendered it necessary, without malice or cruelty, and on the first opportunity took him to Guernsey, preparatory to shipping him for America. At Guernsey he was traced, and when in the hold of an outward-bound vessel, he was pounced on by the Government officers, to whom, it is believed, he had managed to discover himself.

Meanwhile, the dragoons, who had been engaged in the search at home, discovered that, notwithstanding all their caution, their movements were watched, and that intelligence of their approach from Plymouth was sure to precede them to Polperro. A detachment was therefore sent to Truro, with orders to march from the west, in which way they were enabled to come to Polperro unobserved. On one of these visits poor Potter was suprised in his own house, which, unlike most other houses in the place, had no back door leading to the hills, or he might, even then, have escaped. He was taken to London, tried at the Old Bailey, and convicted on the evidence of Roger Toms, which was to the effect that while he, (Toms), was in the cabin, and not actually engaged in the fray, Potter came down, and said, with an oath, that "he had done for one of them". This was enough, as no question could be made of the unlawful resistance, or of the loss of life. Yet this evidence was believed by many to be false, and even impossible. An old coastguardsman, who was engaged in the attack on the lugger, averred that the unfortunate man Bowden was accidentally shot by one of their own crew, and it

"... and carried him off to some place of concealment ..."

was admitted to be a strange circumstance that the shot had entered the man's breast, in a direction opposite to the fire of the smugglers.

After Potter's execution, great as was the pity for him, the desire of revenge was even stronger. Roger Toms was execrated in his native place; even his children learned to detest him, and to this day his name is a term of reproach. His evidence was deemed necessary to convict the other offenders when captured, and he was kept at Newgate on that account for some years. He was also, in all probability, restrained by fear that his life was not safe, except under the immediate protection of the law; so he remained attached to the prison in some menial employment until his death, which happened many years after the date of these occurrences. This is all the Polperro people know, or wish to know about him.

Potter's comrades were perseveringly hunted for a long time, and many stirring tales are told of their escapes; but while a few were punished, the rest contrived to keep out of reach until after the establishment of the coastguard, when a general amnesty appears to have been extended to the offenders.

I might go on to relate many moving adventures, but enough has been said to fulfil my intention—that of presenting Polperro as it was forty or fifty years back. It should be mentioned, however, that in those days the poor-rates were almost nothing, the old and infirm supporting themselves by the sale of smuggled articles which were brought across for them free of freight.

In time of war this dangerous occupation was exchanged for one still more hazardous, and, withal, more profitable. The vessels were commissioned and sent on privateering expeditions, in which their skill and daring rendered our men very successful. It is necessary to relate a few circumstances connected with this service, which have also a bearing on the history of the place.

It was in the time of the first American war, that a privateer was fitted out to cruise against the trade of that country. The French were suspected of rendering private assistance to our enemies, but there was no open rupture between us and our neighbours. When the privateer had been at sea some weeks, she fell in with a Frenchman laden with materials of war; and although she had no commission but that which directed reprisals against the Americans, the prize was taken, after a fight, with the conviction that as matters had been going on for some time past, war with France *must* have been declared by this time. The captain of the privateer knew full well the risk there was of their prize being taken from them on their arrival at Plymoth, if he failed, as he must have done, to show any warrant for this particular act. Accordingly both the privateer and her capture were brought to the harbour of Cork. Here the danger they apprehended was encountered, for, meeting with an English sloop-of-war, a sight of their letters was demanded, and, notwithstanding that the espousal of the American cause by the French had, (as was taken for granted), led to a proclamation of war against the latter power, the prize was taken from them, and a lieutenant was put on

LANDING A CARGO

board as prize-master, while the privateers remained at Cork, sorely disappointed at their loss.

The interests of the Polperro sailors were about this time watched over by a man of singular sagacity and energy, Mr. Zephaniah Job, whose history we must stop a moment to give an account of.

Job was born in the parish of St. Agnes, and received an education that was to fit him for the position of mine-captain, which requires, besides common arithmetic, a knowledge of mensuration and of the lower branches of mathematics. He was, when a very young man, obliged to quit his home abruptly in consequence of some trouble he had brought upon himself in a fit of rage, and so he came to Polperro, where, as a means of subsistence, he undertook to conduct a school. At this time there were no places of instruction except two insignificant charitable institutions; nor was the want much felt, for even people of respectability did not deem it indispensable to have their children taught the arts of reading and writing. Mr. Job's school does not seem to have flourished; but those who had no wish to be taught by him, readily availed themselves of his abilities in another way, and he became their accountant, general correspondent, and adviser in business.

When the privateer of which we were speaking was fitted out, he was appointed to keep her accounts, and, as a reward, was to have a share of the profits without being subject to any of the expenses attending the adventure.

As soon as intelligence of the detention of the prize reached Polperro, Mr. Job bestirred himself, hastened to London, obtained the proper commission against the French, then started for Cork, and, by stratagem or diplomacy, succeeded in re-obtaining the prize, which was forthwith taken to Plymouth. There was no doubt the privateer had performed a public service, and it seemed hard to be deprived of their hardly-earned money, through an informality in the circumstances of the capture. The prize was sold and either as his share, or with it an additional reward for his services, Job received £500, which laid the foundation of his fortune. From this time he became the accountant of most of the smuggling companies of Polperro, and the agent for receiving the sums due to the merchants of Guernsey; and it is a proof of his prudence that though acting for smugglers at a time when the business was a very successful one, he never joined them, and, except in the present instance, had no share in the risks or profits of privateering. He turned his attention to general business, and was prosperous in it. After a while, for his own convenience rather than profit, he established a bank, from which he issued his own notes, those of one or two pounds payable at his own establishment, and those for larger sums at the house of Christopher Smith, alderman of London. He continued to amass money, and lived in very respectable style until his death, when he left a good fortune to his administrators. He owned the lease of Killiow and Colmans, and had the fee-simple of the harbour and quays. He was instrumental in giving the town daily postal communication with Liskeard, the principal post-office of the district.

37

The following three anecdotes have been communicated to me by Mr. H. L. Rowett, who carefully recorded them from living testimony:

"About the beginning of the present century, the Revenue cutter *Providence*, in which were Stephen George, Henry Johns, and several others belonging to Polperro, was caught either by the coastguard or another Revenue cutter in the very act of smuggling, near Fowey: upon which the *Providence* was tried, and condemned by the courts as a smuggler. Having passed through the process of being sold by auction from the Revenue Service to the Admiralty, her name was changed to the *Grecian*, and all the crew were sent, as a punishment, in the same vessel to the West Indies. Here, they shortly fell in with a pirate; the breeze being dull at the time, they lowered their boat to attack her, upon which the pirate was run aground a considerable distance off shore, and her crew tried to escape in the boats; however, just before landing, they were overtaken, when a hand-to-hand fight took place in the surf, up to their knees in water. Many of the pirates were killed, and the remainder, who were all taken prisoners, were conveyed to Jamaica, where they were eventually hung. For this gallant conduct the crew of the *Grecian* were all given their freedom, and permitted to return home to their families".

"One day, during the French war, William Quiller (*b.* 1790, *d.*1823), happened to be in Plymouth without his "Protection", which at that time was granted to the possessors of property, and also to those in trade, exempting them from serving in the navy. The leader of a press-gang, seeing that he was a strong and well-built man, gave orders to seize him, and in spite of his struggles he was soon overcome and taken on board a frigate just on the point of sailing for Jamaica. Shortly after setting sail the names of the crew were called over, to which each man answered, but on Quiller's name being called, he was ordered to stand aside. The late Captain Whitter, R.N., who was in command, then questioned him as to who he was; and, finding him to be the son of an old friend, he appointed him to the quarter-deck, where he soon manifested a smartness and superior ability, that were apparent to all. At Jamaica the ship was attacked by yellow fever, then raging in the island; and by the time the vessel completed her stay there, all the superior officers, including the captain, had either died, or been invalided home, thus leaving William Quiller in command of the frigate after having been on board her only twenty months. He then proceeded to bring her home, which he accomplished in safety. After this, Quiller was appointed to the command of the hired ketch *Gleaner*, which was used as an armed despatch vessel; on one of his voyages, about the year 1814, he came in sight of a Spanish man-of-war, considerably larger than his own vessel, which carried 60 men; the other, as was afterwards found out, being manned by a crew of upwards of three hundred. After a sharp fight, notwithstanding the disparity in size and numbers, Captain Quiller succeeded in boarding the Spaniard and capturing her; she was brought safely to port, and his share of the prize-money was £2,000. The *Gleaner* was afterwards driven ashore in a severe storm off Corunna simultaneously with the retreat of Sir John Moore".

"Mr. Richard Rowett, (*b.* 1770), of Polperro, during the French war commanded the *Unity*, a hired armed lugger; and, when cruising in

38

the Channel, off Ushant, he was very much surprised to find himself one morning at dawn between two frigates, one on either side, who hoisted English colours, but from their build and rig he had his suspicions as to their nationality. All doubts, however, were dispelled, when a shot was fired across his bows to bring him to; and both immediately displayed the French flag. The nearest hailed him, and, considering the *Unity* to be their prize, ordered her to lie to whilst they boarded her. This order Captain Rowett feigned to obey, and for the moment shortened sail; but when under the lee of the enemy, who were both lying to, quite contentedly lowering their boats, with their sails aback, he suddenly spread all sail, passing straight ahead of both frigates, took the helm himself, ordered the crew to lie flat on the deck to escape the perfect shower of balls rained from the bow-chasers and muskets of the enemy, which in their anger and disappointment of so unexpectedly losing their prey, were fired upon them. The *Unity* soon escaped out of range without any one being hurt, and with only very slight damage being done to the sails and rigging, and had the satisfaction of seeing the Frenchmen occupied for a considerable time in trimming and spreading their sails for the pursuit, whilst they were at a safe distance. Being close hauled by the wind, they were soon on the weather bow, and by breakfast time far on the weather gauge of both the heavy lumbering frigates, with their seven hundred Frenchmen, vainly trimming every stitch of canvass. Eventually the pursuit was given up. Thus the little lugger, by a dash unknown in the French navy, had first escaped capture, and then destruction from the heavy broadsides of two frigates. This was considered one of the most daring and brilliant exploits of its kind during the war, and earned for the crew of the *Unity* much praise on all sides. Instead of being captured, and the crew pining in a French prison, this little lugger took many merchantmen as prizes, even at the very mouth of their harbours; and the crew, who were all Polperro men, often returned to their families, and to re-ship those whom they had sent ashore as prize crews".

I now come to the story of Robert Jeffrey, which, at the time of its occurrence, made considerable stir in England.

In 1807, the year of the treacherous peace of Tilsit, privateering was carried on very briskly at Polperro. Among other vessels, the *Lord Nelson*, a fast-sailing schooner, sailed from this port, manned by a crew of hardy and experienced sailors. After cruising in the Channel for a week or more without success, she put into Falmouth for provisions. Our privateers, when under the protection of letters of marque, were constantly liable to the depredations of English ships of war which, against law, of course, and often in a manner scarcely warranted by the exigencies of the time, boarded them at sea or in harbour, and impressed the best of their crews. The *Lord Nelson* was in this way boarded by the *Recruit*, whilst in Falmouth harbour, and deprived of several of her men and boys. Amongst them was Robert Jeffrey, whose story it is our present purpose to tell.

Robert had learnt the craft of a blacksmith from his step-father, well known at Polperro for his ingenuity and skill, but had left it for the more attractive occupation of a sailor, and shipped himself on board the

Lord Nelson. He was pressed, as has been related, into the *Recruit,* a sloop-of-war commanded by Captain Lake, a profligate and reckless young officer; and the latter vessel immediately set sail for the West Indies. Whilst cruising in the Caribbean Sea, Jeffrey, who had been appointed armourer's mate, was accused, and truly, of having got at a barrel of spruce beer intended for the captain's own palate. He might have urged in defence that the pangs of thirst made the temptation too great for the ship's water had for some time been so low, that only a small quantity was served out to each man daily; but the captain had dined, and was not in a fit state for expostulation. Jeffrey was ordered on deck, and accused of the theft. "Lower the boat instantly", cried Captain Lake, "I'll have no thieves on board my ship! Lieutenant Mould, you see that rock? Man a boat, and set the rascal adrift on it". With some little hesitation, expressed more in manner than by words, the boat was lowered and manned, and Jeffrey was taken to the rock. It was dark night when they unbound the youth; but though it was necessary to make all haste back to the ship, it was some time before they could summon sufficient sternness to disregard his passionate entreaties and prayers. At length he found himself alone on this desolate spot, without food; having only a handkerchief, a knife, and a piece of wood which had been humanely given him by his comrades for the purpose of signalling any passing ship. The place on which he was left was the island of Sombrero, one of the Leeward group, desolate and treeless, a naked lump of rock, with no springs or brooks, and, happily perhaps, uninhabited, except by the sea-fowl which roosted in its crags. It was some time before Jeffrey could bring himself to think that the captain meant to do more than intimidate him, and his hope again revived when in the morning light he saw the *Recruit* in the offing. Despair, however, soon succeeded as he saw her fade from his sight, and that nothing was before him but the inhospitable rock, and no less desolate ocean studded with islands. Hunger soon came, and thirst, still less bearable. The spot abounded with sea birds wheeling around him or perching on the rocks, but they were too wary to be caught; and besides these, nothing in the way of food presented itself. He discovered, indeed, an egg, but it was putrid, so that, hungry as he was, it sickened him. The only sustenance he had, if such it could be called, was some bark which the waves had floated to the shore. The salt water, which after a time he was compelled to drink, allayed his immediate cravings, but only served in the end to make them more intense, and he would doubtless have sunk speedily, had not a shower of rain fallen, which collecting in the crevices of the rock, he managed to get at by means of a quill. Several ships appeared at intervals, and he waved his flag in hope of attracting their observation; but they in turn disappeared from his view, leaving him, as our story does for the present, to his hunger and thirst, with the prospect of inevitable death.

The *Recruit,* on leaving the island, steered for Barbadoes to join the squadron under the command of Admiral Sir Alexander Cochrane. The tale of Jeffrey's punishment was whispered about from crew to crew, exciting indignation wherever it was told, until it reached the Admiral's ear, who, severely reprimanding Captain Lake for his brutality, commanded him to return to the rock to rescue the man whom he had so inhumanely abandoned. The time which elapsed between the landing of Jeffrey on the islet, and the return of the *Recruit*, is variously stated. In a narrative of the period it is set down as two months; but a sailor, who was among those impressed from the *Lord Nelson*, and was a witness to the execution of the cruel sentence and the subsequent search for Jeffrey, tells us that little more than a fortnight passed before the *Recruit* was again off Sombrero. A three days search gave no trace of the unfortunate man, the general impression being that he had died a violent death. A pair of trousers, (not Jeffrey's), and a tomahawk handle were the only vestiges of humanity discoverable on this barren spot. The Admiral seems to have been satisfied that the poor fellow had been rescued by some passing ship, and so let the matter rest. The story was however so widely circulated that it at length attracted attention at home, and, even after two years had passed, was agitated with so much spirit that Captain Lake was brought to a court-martial, and dismissed the service. Whilst this was passing, the greatest uncertainty existed as to Jeffrey's fate; and the public were not to be satisfied with any measure of justice short of his restitution, if alive, to his home and family; or the fullest inquiry into the particulars of his fate. His wrongs, therefore, continued to be loudly commented on in the newspapers; and in the House of Commons, Sir Francis Burdett, then very popular, kept the case so perseveringly before the Government, that an order was made for the strictest search.

In this state of anxious uncertainty as to Jeffrey's fate, some hope, not unmingled with doubt, was excited by a statement made on affidavit before the Mayor of Liverpool, by one George Hassel, mariner, who deposed to having seen, at Beverley, in the State of Massachusetts, a youth bearing the name, and answering to the description of Jeffrey. "And the deponent further saith that this Jeffrey was well known in the neighbourhood of Marblehead and Beverley, and was generally called by the name of the 'Governor of Sombrero', it being notoriously known that he had been put on shore by the order of the captain of an English sloop-of-war".

Other facts confirmatory of Hassel's statement came from various quarters, and the proof was supposed to be complete, when an account was received, signed by Jeffrey's own hand, of all that had befallen him since the time of his abandonment on the rock. This paper, intended to set the public mind at rest as to his life and safety, had however the opposite effect of increasing its doubts, for the signature was found to be a cross, whereas the missing man was known to have written a fair hand. A letter from Jeffrey's mother, which appeared in the *Times* (Oct. 4, 1809), asserted her conviction, that this statement was a fabrication by Capt. Lake and his emissaries, and that some one had been suborned to personate her son. To settle the matter finally, a ship was despatched to bring him home, and he arrived at Portsmouth, in October, 1810, three years after his adventure on the island of Sombrero.

I shall now conclude the account of Jeffrey's stay on the desert rock. On the ninth day of his desolation, a vessel approached near enough to notice the signal which he had barely strength enough to make, and it was with a bounding heart that he saw a boat steering towards the rock. The boat which rescued him belonged to the American schooner *Adams*. "He was", says John Dennis, the master, "extremely reduced and exhausted, so as not to be able to speak". He was most kindly treated by the crew of the *Adams*, and soon recovered from his perilous condition.

He was taken to Marblehead, where his distressing story excited active sympathy, and there he remained maintaining himself by his labours at the forge, quite ignorant of the interest his fate was exciting in England, and, it must be added, culpably forgetful of the unhappiness his friends must be suffering in his Cornish home.

On his arrival in England the Admiralty gave him his discharge, and he was immediately taken, under the care of a naval officer, to Polperro, and delivered to his overjoyed relatives and friends.

There was much rejoicing at Polperro on his return. Almost all the villagers turned out and welcomed the lost one with music and merriment. "The meeting between the mother and her son", says a contemporary account, "was extremely affecting and impassioned".

It was not overlooked that, besides the punishment Captain Lake had already undergone, he was still open to civil or criminal process in a court of law, and Jeffrey was accordingly communicated with by an agent of the noble family concerned, and overtures were made, accompanied by expressions of regret and sympathy evidently unfeigned. He wisely consented to forego any further prosecution of the matter on the payment of six hundred pounds.

It would have been his wisest plan now, to have settled down quietly in his home, and occupied himself in his trade; but he was induced by some traders in notoriety, and a few foolish though well-meaning neighbours, to turn to profit the interest with which his adventures had invested him and he proceeded to London, where, showing himself on the boards of some of the minor theatres, "Jeffrey the Sailor" was for a time one of the sights of the town. After a few months he returned to Polperro with money enough to purchase a small schooner intended for the coasting trade. The speculation was unsuccessful; Jeffrey fell into consumption, and died, leaving a wife and daughter in great poverty.

At the beginning of the present century smuggling was carried on so daringly, and to such an extent as to call for better organised means to repress it. Captures were frequent, and the law was rigorously enforced on all offenders. Officers were appointed on this service whose business it was to get an intimate knowledge of our creeks and coves, and a boat and crew were stationed at Polperro; and this, I have been told, was the germ of the Preventive or Coastguard Service, now one of the permanent institutions of the land. Their duties, as regards the prevention of smuggling, have become light, but they will be always valuable as a reserve force. This Polperro preventive boat was the first in Cornwall and, it is said, in England.

These determined measures for the extinction of the "free trade" struck consternation in the minds of all engaged in it; but, though active opposition was not politic, the people determined one and all, to offer as much passive resistance as was safe. No one would let a coastguard-man a house to live in at any price; so the whole force was obliged to make a dwelling and guard-house of the hull of a vessel which was moored to the old quay. In no long time the contraband trade became too dangerous to be profitable, antipathies wore out, the preventive men made themselves agreeable to the people they had come amongst, and were admitted to the town. At the present those prejudices have so completely died out, that it is an object of ambition to the young sailors of Polperro to get admission to that service which was to their grand-fathers an object of bitter hatred, and perhaps there is scarcely another place which has furnished it with so many men. It is also remarkable that however they may be dispersed, they invariably, when age or infirmity pensions them, come back to their native valley to end their days.

5

THE PEOPLE AND THEIR OCCUPATIONS

As far as Polperro is concerned, I should, speaking roughly, say that two-thirds of its people are engaged in fishing and other maritime pursuits, and the other third in agriculture, trade, and commerce.

Our fishermen are a hardy race of men, often leading a life of no little peril and privation. They are often accused by those who know them little, of being reckless and thriftless; but much may be said in exculpation, for their gains are rarely considerable, and at all times precarious; whilst the expenses of the craft are constant and pressing. It is then scarcely to be wondered at that, during the storms of winter, (sometimes long continued), their little stock should be exhausted and imminent starvation threaten them. A good stock of potatoes from the garden or plot upon the cliff, and well-filled steans of salted pilchards, much help to avert it. It is to be regretted, however, that fishermen do not see the possibility of employing their time, when stormy weather prevents them from going to sea or profitably following their occupation, in some work connected with their calling, as the making of nets, or the spinning of lines. Notwithstanding the obvious advantage of such a course, they continue to buy their nets at Bridport, instead of employing on them their own spare time, and that of their wives and children, who can *mend* nets very adroitly, which is a more difficult task than making them. A large item might be thus saved in their expenditure.

They compare ill with other craftsmen in respect of book-learning, but are remarkably shrewd and sagacious in all matters pertaining to their avocation, and are endowed with more than an average share of natural wit. Tenacious of their rights, and firmly attached to old customs, they are not easily persuaded to adopt improvements, even when these obviously recommend themselves. As an instance of this, it is only within the last five or six years that they have provided themselves with a cuddy or locker in the bows of their boats; up to which time they were content to coil in sleep at the bottom with no other covering than their thick sea-dress and a coarse tarpaulin. Another alteration for the better, slightly older than this, is the practice of sinking the drift nets to some depth below the surface, in order to avoid danger from ships running across them; a method which seems to have been in use in Norway in remote times.

They are brave and intrepid, and in cases of shipwreck, or distress at sea, have been seen to run great hazard, when the prospect of danger was great, and of gain very little. The stories of wreckers, which writers of *fiction* are so fond of perpetuating, could not within a long remembrance, have been told of this neighbourhood. That our people may be found occasionally in time of wreck to carry off property which the waves may cast ashore, being uninstructed in the laws of jettsom and flottsom, I will not deny; but their hospitality to the shipwrecked has often been as remarkable as the ingratitude not unfrequently shown by those whom they have saved, fed, and clothed from their scanty stores.

And now of fishing; its various modes, and the several sorts of fish which are most the object of the fisherman's pursuit.

We have about thirty fishing-boats, besides punts engaged during the spring and summer in taking lobsters and crabs. The former class are employed in the hook-and-line, and drift-net fisheries. They are of smaller size than those of Mevagissey and Mount's Bay, and adapted to the present condition of the harbour; about twenty-seven feet in the keel, and from nine to ten feet in the beam, and clinker-built. Remarkably stiff for their size, they are, when well-handled, fast-sailing and safe. In ordinary times they carry but one mast, which has a sprit-mainsail and gaff top-sail; also a forestay fastened to an iron beak on the stem, and carrying a foresail. They frequently hoist, besides, a mizen, and rig out a bowsprit and jib. There is no deck, excepting the small cuddy between the first beam and the stem, and they are scantily furnished with a binnacle-box with its compass, and some rude contrivance for holding a fire. Often in the calm weather of summer, beneath a burning sun, the fishermen have to pull this heavy boat to and from the fishing grounds, ten or fifteen miles off. In time of hook-fishing the crew consists of two men; and the catch is divided into fifths, of which one is the share of the owner of the boat, and the remaining four are divided equally between the two men. Certain sorts of fish, such as dog-fish, ray, skate, gurnard, scad, power, and a few others not generally esteemed for the table, are called *rabble-fish*, and are shared by the fishermen without any share for the boat. Thus the only exclusive profit of the owner, who is frequently master fisherman, is the boat's share. In the driving season the boat is manned by four men, and the proceeds are divided into eight parts, of which the boats and nets take half; the remainder is shared between the crew. A lad usually accompanies them, who is rewarded with what he can save from the losses during the draught by his "kieve net", and by the capture of hake and other fish in the intervals.

The crew of a sean consists of eighteen men and, commonly, a boy. The wages of the ordinary seaner have varied from eight to twelve shillings per week; the men who actually shoot the sean have a shilling a week extra, while the master-seaner's pay is a guinea, with a gratuity on each hundred hogsheads which he is so fortunate as to catch; besides which, the crew are in common entitled to a third part of the fish sold fresh, and a fourth of that which is exported; in some places not even paying for the casks in which they are packed.

The Pilchard is indeed our most important fish, and is caught in seans and drift-nets from July to the end of the year, and are even taken in lesser schulls as late as March. Its capture by the sean is thus managed:

Two boats, flat and not clinker-built like the ordinary fishing boat, are needed. They are usually forty feet long, by ten in breadth of beam, and are accompanied by a third much smaller boat, the *lurker*, in their fishing expeditions. One of the larger boats, the *sean-boat*, carries a net of about two hundred and twenty fathoms in length and twelve in depth, buoyed at top, along the head rope, by a row of corks, and at foot weighted by leads at intervals. A second boat, the *volyer* (a corruption, perhaps, of *follower*), has another sean-net of a hundred or more fathoms in length, and eighteen in depth, differing from the former or *stop-sean* in having a hollow or bunt in the middle.

During the fishery the master seaner has the entire command, and holds himself quite independent even of the adventurers. In August operations commence; and the boats proceed to the neighbouring bay, and anchor; keeping a good look-out for the appearance of fish, which commonly show themselves by a rippling of the surface, *stoiting* or leaping; or by the colour imparted to the sea. When a schull is discovered, the lurker first proceeds to the place to ascertain its magnitude and the direction it is taking. The depth of water, the clearness of the ground from rocks, and the force and course of the tide, enter also into the master's calculation before he makes the signal to prepare. All the proceedings are directed by signs, for the fish are alarmed by noise; and, when everything is favourable, a warp from the end of the stop-sean is handed to the *volyer*, whose duty it is to keep all *taut*; the *lurker* still continuing near the fish, to observe their motions, and to point out to the sean-boat the space to be enclosed. The sean-boat, at this important period, is rowed by four men, the other three being employed in throwing or *shooting* the net, and such is the vigour exerted on the occasion, that this great quantity of net, rope, cork, and lead is thrown into the sea in less than five minutes. The sean, at first forms a curved line across the course of the shoal; and while the larger boats are engaged in warping the ends together, the lurker takes its station in the opening, in order that by dashing the water with the oars, the fish may be kept from the only place where escape is possible. When the sean is closed, and the opposite ends are laced together, if the body of the fish be great, and the sea or tide strong, it is secured in its situation by heavy grapnels, carried off from it in the direction from which the danger is feared.

It will appear, from this account of the method of proceeding, that it is not more difficult to take a thousand hogsheads of fish than a much smaller number; the only difference being that with the larger body the sean is regularly moored; a measure which with the smaller quantity, would be, perhaps, unnecessary. It may even be said that the capture of the larger body is the more easily effected, for as its motion is slower, its course is less speedily changed through alarm from the fishermen. When the tide is low, the next business is to take up the fish. For this purpose, leaving the stop-sean as before, the volyer passes within it, and lays its sean, termed the *tuck*, round the former, on the inner side of its inclosure; the latter is then drawn together so as gradually to contract the limits of the fish, and raise them from the bottom. When disturbed they become exceedingly agitated, and so great is the force derived from their numbers and terror, that the utmost caution is necessary to prevent them from sinking or bursting the net; whilst to hinder their escape back again from the tuck-sean into the stop, stones suspended from ropes, (termed *minnies*), are continually kept plunging opposite the only

46

aperture. By these means, the fish then to be taken up are supported in the hollow or bunt of the tuck-sean, and lifted nearly dry to the surface; the voices of the men being lost in the noise of the fish as they beat the water. This most important part of their task being accomplished, the seaners proceed to fix themselves in pairs on the gunwales of the boats, and with flaskets to *lade* the fish on board; while what is contained in the stop-sean more than the boats are supposed to be able to carry, is left for a future opportunity. It is one principal mark of a good master-seaner that he forms a correct opinion of the quantity enclosed, and is able to take from it into the tuck-sean only just so much as can be properly disposed of in the cellar for that day. It is by the extent of the *briming*, or light excited at night in sea-water by anything that disturbs it, that this judgment is formed; but nothing short of experience can enable any one to form a correct opinion in this particular.

Many are the advantages which result from the practice of taking up only a portion at separate times, when the quantity of fish is considerable, for the whole can thus be salted in a proper condition without fatigue or extraordinary expense; the sean is preserved from the risk of bursting, and the fish from the danger of being killed by the pressure of their own weight; in which case the whole might be lost, together with the sean; since no human force could raise to the surface a thousand hogsheads of fish after life had become extinct. This slow method of proceedings is especially desirable, where the men find it for their interest to sell as much as possible fresh for home consumption. A shoal of pilchards has thus been left even for a week, part being taken up every night. I have been informed of an instance wherein a ship was dispatched to France for salt after the sean was shot, and returned with her cargo soon enough to cure the fish.

The work of curing is performed by women, twelve of whom are employed on one sean. The fish are piled up in order, in *bulk*, against the walls of the cellar, a layer of fish alternately with a layer of salt, and in this state they are allowed to remain for thirty days, the oil and brine being suffered to drain from them into pits prepared for the purpose. They are then taken out and sifted by which means the dry salt is separated from them; then carefully washed in another sieve, and placed in very regular order in casks, each measuring fifty gallons, the staves of which are put together with many crevices, so that the oil on pressure may readily escape. The necessary pressure is effected by levers to which heavy weights are hung; and the casks being thus repeatedly pressed down and refilled for the space of nine days, and until the weight of the barrel is 476 pounds, they are finally headed up for exportation. Each barrel is branded with the curer's name, the date of the year, B.F. for British Fish, and the number 3,000, that being the supposed contents of the hogshead. The oil that escapes from the fish on pressure is carefully attended to, and forms a valuable article of trade.

When seans are engaged in looking for fish, it is usual for them to occupy what are called *turns*, which are certain measured spaces on the fishing grounds, in which the sean that first arrives possesses the exclusive right of fishing for a certain period, after which, whether it has *shot* or not, but sooner, if it has *shot*, even though no fish has been taken, it is superseded by another. These turns are established by law at St. Ives, and might with advantage be generally enforced.

Seaning is not ancient at Polperro, the first being set on foot about the year 1782; for I find first mention made of the exportation of pilchards taken by the *Polperro* in 1783. As our resident fishermen knew nothing of the practical management of a sean, they procured a master from Mevagissey, and, I believe, gave him the sixteenth part of it, called *an ounce*, as his reward, besides his regular wages, and share of captures. Copying the practice of such concerns at his own port, it was he that induced them to pay a composition of £1 6s. 8d. in lieu of tithes to the clergyman of the parish in which the sean was kept. Quarrels arose between the Mevagissey man and his employers, and he left before his second year.

Encouraged by the success of their first adventure, a second sean, the *Gannet*, was soon started, and both were for many years highly prosperous. The seaners of Polperro attained a high reputation for skill, and in the early part of this century were employed in this fishery at Newquay, in North Cornwall; and along the South-coast at Bigbury Bay, Cawsand, Downderry, Seaton, Looe, Polruan, and Fowey. Seaning has miserably declined of late years, and this fishery is abandoned at Polperro. At out neighbouring ports also it struggles against a discouraging want of success.

The fitting out of a sean costs little less than a thousand pounds, and it is also to be observed that the cost in wages and contingencies of keeping it at sea is considerable; but it lasts much longer than a drift net before it needs renewal.

Drift-fishing for the pilchard is of much more ancient date than the sean, as far as Polperro is concerned. The outfit consists of a number of nets, varying according to the means of the fishermen, but usually amounting to about twenty; each net being from eighteen to twenty fathoms in length, and seven fathoms deep; so that a string of driving nets may reach three-quarters of a mile. These nets are fastened to each other in length, and to a head-line, along which runs a row of corks: another line runs loosely along the middle of the nets to afford additional strength in rough weather, or when the nets are drawn. Drift nets are carried on board a common fishing-boat, with an addition to her usual crew; and they are cast or shot at the going down of the sun, to be drawn or *hauled* in about two hours. They are again shot as morning approaches; for pilchards are most active, and enter the nets best, in the morning and evening. A rope from the end of the nets is fastened to the bow of the boat, to be shifted to the quarter when they are hauled; and the string is left to float with the tide, for no sails are set, except in very calm weather, to prevent the nets from folding together. Within a few years an improvement has been made in the method of drift fishing, by which it has been rendered more productive, and hazards are avoided to which the nets were formerly exposed by their getting entangled in the keels and rudders of passing ships. It consists in diminishing the number and size of the corks along the head-line, and in fixing cords at proper distances with a stout buoy of cork affixed to each. By these means the nets are sunk to a depth sufficient to reach the fish when they do not appear on the surface. This mode of fishing has long been in use on the coast of Norway in the herring fishery; and, with us, the drift net has been rendered more successful thereby. When the nets are sunk to the depth of two fathoms it is often found that the foot is still the most productive of fish.

The drift fishery was in a considerable state of prosperity at the time when seans were set on foot; but as the latter became popular from success, they attracted the wealthy owners and best fishermen. In consequence the drift boats diminished in number, so that at last only one was sent to sea from Polperro. Additional reasons for this decline were that the merchants (who were somewhat biassed perhaps by being themselves owners of seans), refused to purchase drift-fish, on the alleged ground that they were less valuable by being caught through *strangling*, and because the success of sean-fishing for the time allowed them greatly to undersell the drift-fisherman. This method of taking the pilchard has again revived, and become a favourite; so that seventeen boats from this harbour are engaged in its prosecution; and, in the intervals of this special fishery, they go to east and west in pursuit of herrings.

In the open sea, drift-nets are commonly cast in the direction of the tide, because they are thus most easily kept in a straight course; but when near the shore, or at the entrance of a bay, the favourite position is parallel to its direction, by which means the fish are intercepted in their advance or retreat. But the importance of shooting as much as possible *across the tide* will appear from the fact that I have seen drift boats cast their nets in the midst of a multitude of fish, one in the direction of the tide, and the other across it; and in less than two hours, the former caught nothing, and the latter nine thousand.

The most successful time for driving is in hazy weather with some motion of the waves, but in clear moonlight the fish are shy; and in very dark nights, the briming makes the nets look like a wall of fire, and deters the fish.

During the Pilchard Fishery, if it be successful, Polperro presents a very busy scene; and with reason; for no other employment diffuses its blessings so widely. The boon to the pauper with his weekly half-a-crown is very great; for a half-penny will supply him with a savoury and nutritious meal. The method of preparing them for home use is by breaking off the head, and scooping out the entrails with the finger, in doing which our women are exceedingly quick and neat. The fish are then washed, lined with salt, and placed in a well-tightened barrel or eathenware pot; a layer of fish alternating with a layer of salt; and thus they become covered with brine as the salt dissolves; a circumstance judged necessary to their proper preservation. Thus prepared, salt pilchards are esteemed a necessary part of the provision of every family, but especially among the poor. For immediate consumption they are *scrawed*, that is gutted, split, powdered with salt and pepper, and hung in the sun. When broiled after this process they form a favourite food.

The cost of the outfit of a boat and nets for driving may amount to two hundred and fifty pounds. The price of each net of the string is about six pounds, and it is usually supposed to last about six years; requiring, however, frequent mending from damages done by predatory fishes, and especially the blue-shark, which almost regularly attends these nets, and proceeds from one end of them to the other, cutting out fish at its pleasure, and swallowing them together with the portion of the net that holds them.

The greatest number captured by one boat within my experience was 40,000; but I have been informed on credible testimony of 80,000 being taken in a single capture.

The Conger is frequently caught at from ten to fifteen leagues from land, on sandy bottoms. The colour of the fish is then white, and its size enormous; in some cases exceeding a hundred weight. In our littoral gullies, their colour is a rich purplish black; and this variety is caught by an arrangement of hooks and lines locally termed *boultys* or *boulters*, consisting of a long line, having, at intervals of two fathoms, a snood of five or six feet long, armed with a tinned hook. This boulty is stretched and moored, and its position marked by a buoy. The snoods have many separate cords, to prevent the fish easily liberating itself by gnawing the line. Baited with cuttle or pilchard this plan is very successful for the black or shore congers. This fish is undervalued as food among the better classes, but finds a quick sale at a low price among the poorer people. A proclivity to pies is said to be among the characteristics of the Cornish, and a conger pie, properly made, is no contemptible dish. This fish was specially prepared for exportation as early as the time of King John; and within living memory a considerable trade was carried on at Polperro in what was called "conger douce", probably sweet conger, which was largely exported to Spain, Portugal, and the coasts of the Mediterranean. It was thus prepared: The fish were cut flat through their length, and sewn together with twine so as to form a continuous sheet, then stretched on a frame-work, without salt, or other preservative, until they were dried. In wet seasons much loss, and more offence to the noses of the towns-people, accrued from so very coarse a process; but when properly prepared, it was considered a great delicacy by our continental neighbours, when grated in their soup. The conger newly taken were purchased by the fish-curers at a price rarely so high as five shillings per cwt., and although there was immense loss in this rude drying process, it often sold for thirty shillings per cwt. This trade fell into disuse during the wars of the French Revolution, but chiefly on account of the scarcity of the fish, for the Conger has not for many years been caught in sufficient quantity to satisfy the market at home, and consequently fetches a higher price than could be obtained for it as conger douce.

Tithe of fish was paid to the rector of Lansallos down to a late date; but the constant shifting of the fisherman's residence across the brook into Talland, made its levy, often disputed, not worth the trouble, and Mr. Pooley on this account allowed his claim to lapse.

The Agriculture of the district has little that is characteristic; but a few facts may hereafter, if not now, be thought worthy of the record.

Our two parishes are hilly, and very various in the quality and value of the soil; in some places easy of cultivation, and rendering grateful return; in others so steep that they are indebted to the modern introduction of artificial manures, of easy carriage, for their tillage.

The average annual rent of land is about a pound per acre. We have no common, and scarcely any waste or uncultivated land; for even down our precipitous cliffs the fisherman varies his sea-faring pursuits by cultivating his potato plot ; to the detriment perhaps of the picturesque character of the scenery. The hills along the sea-side are used for the pasturage of sheep, and are occasionally torn up and tilled, in order to renew the pasture. There is very little of irrigation or drainage, the first being generally impracticable, and the porous nature of the subsoil rendering the second unnecessary.

The ground is manured chiefly with farm-yard dung, and the *ore weed* which the storms of winter throw upon the beach. In modern times guano and the various artificial fertilizers have been largely used, but chiefly for green crops.

Wheat and barley are the staple produce; oats being only grown in limited quantities for consumption by the horses on the homestead. Potatoes at one time were cultivated to an extent which was excluding other crops; but the inscrutable disease which made its appearance in 1845, and, unhappily, continues, has much lessened their culture.

Our bullocks are chiefly of the North Devon breed, with a little admixture of the Durham, and our dairy cows are generally of the ordinary, but occasionally of the Jersey sort. The sheep are mostly South-hams; the pure Leicester being too delicate to stand the exposure to the winds and rains of our weather-beaten coast.

The cottage labourer is as ill-housed as in the neighbouring parishes; but in this respect improvement is to be observed, and the old cob-walled and thatched cottage is giving way to a more commodious house, built of native stone and covered with Delabole slate. The usual rent of such a cottage is from two to three pounds yearly.

Up to a later period the wages of a day labourer were eighteen pence a day, but in consequence of the rapid emigration during the last three or four years, and other circumstances, such as the better remuneration of a sea-faring life, the able farm-labourer gets two shillings a day, and the settlement is monthly. If a man works steadily at a place, he takes a portion of his wages in corn at a stated price, which, taking all fluctuations of the market into the account, is generally fair. Male servants in the house are hired for the year, and their wages used to be about eight pounds; now, however, ten, and even twelve pounds are given. The yearly wages of a servant girl are from four to five pounds. Besides these most farmers have an extra man for a month in harvest-time.

51

The system of farming at present in vogue may be simply described as three years in tillage, and three years out in pasture. Land broken for wheat is *thwarted* in the Spring, being ploughed down concentrically, so as to leave, here and there, a very narrow rib called a "comb". The gress being thus turned downwards by the plough is directed to the line of the comb and rotted. The comb is useful in offering resistance to the harrow, and disengaging the turf which would otherwise accumulate on the "tens" or teeth. If an old grass field with a thick face is to be taken into culture, the skimming plough is used, and the process is called "felling". The turf is collected into separate "burrows", or heaps, burnt, and the ashes "scoaded", or scattered over the field. Occasionally before breaking the land a number of parallel furrows are driven across it; the upturned earth, and the clearing of the hedge-gripe, being carried to heaps at certain distances apart, generally five to an acre. This earth is useful in triturating and dividing the manure, which is carted to these heaps, and mixed. The dung thus made is wheeled into smaller heaps, spread, and ploughed in; after which the ground is harrowed and sown. After wheat-harvest the "Arish", or stubble, remains until spring, when it is broken up for turnips or mangel-wurzel: and afterwards sown with barley and grass seeds, to be mown for hay, and finally go out of tillage for a fallow of three years. There is very little corn stacked out in the fields as in some places. It is generally taken to the homestead and made into oblong mows in an enclosure named the mowhay. In uncertain harvest-weather the sheaves are hastily put into small arish-mows in the field, the grain ends meeting at the centre, and arranged roof-like at the top. By this plan the grain will stand heavy and continuous rains without damage; and are taken to the mowhay when opportunity serves.

The use of oxen for draught is fast going out; but it was a common thing a few years since to see two or even three yoke dragging lazily the plough through the furrow, while the plough-boy drove them with a goad, or encouraged them by a measured chant, (the sweetest of our rural sounds), in which the names of the oxen, "Spark and Beauty, Brisk and Lively, Good-Luck and Speedwell" might be distinguished. Now oxen are reared only for the market. There must have been a great deal of useless force thus expended, as the farm only needs its former number of horses, though the labouring oxen have been dismissed. Now it is more common to see the ploughman holding his plough, drawn by a pair of horses, which he directs himself by two reins, dispensing with the ploughboy and his goad; and it is certain that field-work is thus much more quickly dispatched.

As a general rule our orchards supply the farms with cider, and very little is sold or exported. Lately screw cider-presses have been introduced, but until recently the lever press was used to squeeze out the juice from the alternate layers of pulped apple and reed termed the "cheese". The apples are pounded by a hand-mill; but the older method was by crushing them in a circular granite trough by a roller of the same material drawn round by a horse.

Polperro had never any local government apart from that of the two parishes, and consequently there are no town archives to consult.

the house and the garden, besides useful receipts, pleasant tales, foreign adventures, enigmas, and rebuses; the latter two usually answered, and in verse, in following numbers, made very pleasing and useful reading. These papers were not sent by post as now, but by private messengers hired to "ride Sherborne"; that is, to scour the country on horseback, bestriding their saddle bags, and as they went from place to place to distribute the papers, collect the money and take fresh orders. The fame of the newspaper survived until very lately, for a gossip and newsmonger was spoken of as "a regular Sherborne".

An Astrologer.—In the year 1849 died, at the age of ninety-two, John Stevens, an astrologer. He was a shoemaker, a man of solitary habits, very studious, as you would judge by his look and gait, and considered generally to be above the average run of people in his station. If his good-will was obtained he would employ his art in foretelling the fates of his neighbours, expecting for his labour neither fee nor reward. He was said to have predicted many things accurately, such as the date of the inquirer's death, and whether or not certain persons would recover from the sickness under which they were then labouring. He failed, however, in forecasting his own future; a fact which was accounted for by his advanced age and failing faculties. After his death his library was found to consist of Ephemerides, and other books on the science of the stars and their government of human actions; some in quarto, and in black letter, but none that were thought very curious. In a round shallow box were found three plates of brass, which, when combined, he had called an orrery, having engraved on them representations of tables and diagrams of planetary motions. One of these plates was a dissected circle with astronomical signs and constellations, and a central hole, in which had been a fixed a wire. By moving this over the area he traced the conjunctions of planets, and so resolved the horoscope of the person consulting. His daughter stated that within her knowledge this instrument had cost him in repairs, twenty-four shillings, which was a large sum to a man in his station in life. The instrument cannot be clearly described here, but it was evidently a philosophical arrangement of great complexity and skill, that from its look must have been the work of a maker of some eminence in a past day when astrology was much more trusted in than at present. Besides this apparatus there were several others made by himself, and not copied from any discoverable source. They were very intricate, and showed no little astronomical knowledge; being diagrams of circles and ellipses, partly fixed and partly moveable, with strings fixed in the centre which by their intersections denoted the planetary conjunctions. John Stevens was no Whachum

> "To be an under-conjuror.
> Or journeyman astrologer",

but skilful as well as sincere in the exercise of his science. The worst effect of it on him was that it led him to exclude God and His providence from the world, and to substitute the stars and an unavoidable fate. He was far in intellect above the ordinary conjuror and discoverer of witcheries and thefts, who was plainly an imposter, knowing no more than his neighbours except how best to impose on their credulity. Harry Warne was one of the latter kind, a clever fellow, no mean mathematician, and capable of better things. He had not really the slightest faith in his craft, but the public at large had great trust in him, and he had the skill to use his influence. Harry was a lazy fellow, who deemed any reasonable way of getting a living better than work. His visits to the neighbouring farm-houses were not unwelcome, because he could "turn his hand to anything", and was, moreover, a merry companion. One morning he dropped in on a farmer, and for his dinner engaged to spin some straw for thatching. By meal-time Harry had spun two bundles of such very large size, that super-natural aid was suspected; but at all events he was more than usually welcome to his dinner. Soon after this the same farmer had to call in Harry's aid as conjuror to find out who had stolen his two missing pack-saddles. The oracular reply was, "They'll be found after harvest", a prediction which turned out true, for on using the two prodigious bundles of rope in thatching the mow they too soon disclosed themselves.

Domestic Usages.—Up to the middle of the last century wood and furze were the only fuel. Mr. Bartlett, a merchant, and no unimportant man among us in his day, exported corn and other country produce largely, and imported Plymouth limestone and Welsh culm to make lime for the farmer. Kilns were built, and a good trade was done in this way; for before this the calcareous manure had been obtained by dredging the sea-sand from Talland and Lantivet bays, and lodging them, chiefly, at *Sand-quay*. With the culm, Mr. Bartlett brought over some coal for his own domestic use, and the town slowly adopted it, at first as only supplementary to the wood fire, which it soon almost completely displaced, and now it has become a necessity for the town, and a source of considerable trade, for the old brakes at Talland-sand-hill and elsewhere have been long torn up, and tilled in a more remunerative way. The large fire-places in our old houses have been narrowed to suit modern convenience, and the brake which was considered indispensable, even to each separate farm, has generally disappeared. In the time of wood fires it was the custom to bake the bread by placing the well-kneaded dough on the capacious hearth-stone, covering it with an eathenware pan, and burying it in the glowing embers. The bread thus baked was nicely cooked and palatable, the crust not hard, and the whole spongy. After this it became the custom for each house to have its own earthenware oven, heated by the furze faggot, but soon the common bake-house came in, a convenient spot to which the assembled dames brought their bread and pies, and loitered a little while over a free comment on the affairs of neighbours. It was also the custom not long since for women to take the corn to mill, see it ground, and bring home their grist; for, rightly or wrongly, millers have ever been a suspected race. Honest ones are popularly known, being distinguished by some mark or tuft of hair in the palm of the hand. Accordingly the Polperro housewives, like the two clerks of Cantebregge, were accustomed for

> "*a litel stound*
> *To go to melle and see here corne i grounde*",

and, as the quantity was small, to carry it home. Hence several women would be waiting for their turn at the mill, which, like the bake-house, became a noted centre of scandal. A bit of doubtful gossip was proverbially termed "a mill-house story". The sale of bread, except as penny-loaves, Easter and hot-cross buns, was unknown in these times.

Weaving.—It was the custom of our forefathers, continued to a time included by the memory of elderly people, but now quite gone out, to card, spin, and weave their own hose, blankets, and cloth. Weaving occupied the after hours of some skilled labourers and their families. The last to follow this employment was Fiddick, of Adam's-hill, on the Landaviddy estate. The loom and shuttle used might now be esteemed clumsy instruments, but they were effective ones. Mr. George Coath, of Penhellick, in Pelynt, and afterwards the purchaser of Rafiel, was a woolcomber and weaver, as was also Mr. Ralph Powne, of Tremeere. Women at their homes, were profitably employed, when household duties permitted, in carding and spinning with their *turns* the wool supplied to them; and the yarn was afterwards sent to the local loom to be sent out as blanket, or coarse frieze. No dyes were used but those of Nature's production, for it was a piece of good husbandry to keep a black sheep or two, whose wool spun in certain proportion with the white fleece made a coarse but substantial grey hose, which had the great merit of not soon showing soilure. The young people of Polperro probably have never seen carding or spinning, but another employment which has taken its place is the knitting of blue Guernsey frocks and stockings of worsted supplied from Plymouth. The proceeds of this labour used to be taken up on a most reprehensible *truck* system.

Parish 'prentices.—Before the present poor-law regulations were instituted, our poorer fishermen and others driven to distress by a long run of untoward weather, would now and then, in droves, apply to the parish overseer for temporary relief, occasionally without necessity. The overseer was asked by the applicant to be furnished with employment, and the poor man was sent to a farmer in the parish to ask for work. In the case of a fisherman, his services in agriculture were of little value, so he travelled often from farm to farm vainly seeking for a job, and in some cases, perhaps not anxiously desiring one. Returning from his bootless journey, he demanded from the overseer a day's wages for doing really nothing. It was also the custom for the overseer to insist, before granting relief, that the children of sufficient age should be sent out as apprentices among the farmers and the ratepayers; the masters binding themselves to give them proper sustenance and clothing until the age of twenty-one years in case of a boy, and eighteen in a girl, in consideration of their services. Lots were drawn for the children under the inspection and authority of the magistrates, sitting in their petty-sessional division; each ratepayer being allotted them in proportion to his rating, and the number he already had. The poor boys and girls thus got a settlement, and when the apprenticeship expired they claimed to have employment found for them at a regulated price. There are still some ratepayers who hold that this rude system worked well, and that it produced a servant, steady, honest, careful of his master's interest, and so attached to his family as to go through a long life without change of place.

Light.—"Meat, money, and light, all in one night" was an old proverb applied to a good catch of pilchards, but the reference to the last mentioned commodity is almost forgotten. The light of the fisherman's house was derived from an earthenware or tin lamp filled with train oil from the pilchard, and fitted with a wick supplied by the pith of the common rush, which was deftly peeled of its outer skin, and kept in bundles for the purpose. This rather ill-smelling contrivance is now gone out of use, though forty years ago it was common. The flint and steel and tinder box are now no more, having given way to the handier, but scarcely more reliable, lucifer match.

Wedding, Birth etc.—When a wedding occurs, there being no bells to ring in honour of the occasion, it is usual to call the fowling-pieces into requisition for a *feu de joie*, the ammunition being provided at the cost of the bridegroom. Next day, not knowing of honeymoon or bridal trip, the husband puts on again his fishing attire and resumes his ordinary work. At weddings and christenings it was formerly the custom, when the party set out for church, for one person to be sent before with a piece of bread or cake in his or her hand, (a woman was usually selected for the office), and this was presented to the first person met in the procession. The gift was called the *Kimbly*, and was also given, at births, to the person who brought the first news to those interested in the new arrival.

I might go on to speak of changes in social manners, and the introduction of comforts, now deemed necessaries, but I must hold my hand, though I believe their record might be found interesting hereafter.

7

POPULAR ANTIQUITIES—FAIRY MYTHOLOGY

It will have been seen that our town has few, if any, material remains connecting it with the story of our common land. The ages have glided by it without noise, leaving no marks of their flow. Its small importance, its seclusion, and the unambitious lives of its inhabitants, gave it but little community of interest with the world outside. We have therefore no vestiges of ecclesiastical grandeur, or tall towers bearing the dints of conflict, to show the antiquary; but we have stores of what will be only a little less interesting to him, remnants of faded creeds, curious customs, and fragments of earlier conditions of society. In this quiet corner lurk many relics of the "fair humanities of old religion", many an ancient usage whose origin and intention are scarcely to be guessed at. They have quite vanished from places more subject to change, along with the circumstances which gave rise to them, but they are still retained here; just as the side eddy of the stream detains sticks and straws which the current would have swept off to the ocean. I attempted to save them long ago, on account of the fancy contained in them, and the rich poetic light which age had cast about them; having at the time little notion that they were valuable in showing community of fable, and thereby aiding ethnology and language in tracing the origin, migrations, and relationships of a people, where written history could not aid us.

Polperro is rich in remains of Fairy Mythology, and I shall here give some of the tales which are still, or were until very lately, told by the peasantry with a sort of half belief.

The belief in the little folk is far from dead among us, although the people of this generation hold it by a slighter tenure than their forefathers did, and are aware that piskies are now fair objects of ridicule, whatever they may formerly have been. One old women in particular, to whose recital of some of the following tales I have listened in mute attention, was a firm believer in them; and I well remember her pettish reply when a young friend of mine ventured to hint a doubt: "What! not believe in mun, when my poor mother heth been pinched black and blue by mun?" The argument was conclusive to us, for we could not then see its fallacy, though we have since learnt that the poor soul in question had not the kindest of husbands.

This creed has received so many additions and modifications at one time, and has suffered so many abstractions at another, that it is impossible to make any arrangement of our fairies into classes. "The elves of hills, brooks, standing lakes, and groves" are all now confounded under the generic name *pisky*. Some of the later interpolations are of a very obvious character, as will hereafter be pointed out. Our piskies are little beings standing midway between the purely spiritual and the material, suffering a few, at least, of the ills incident to humanity. They have the power of

59

POLPERRO.

making themselves seen, heard, and felt. They interest themselves in man's affairs; now doing him a good turn, anon taking offence at a trifle, and leading him into all manner of mischief. The rude gratitude of the husbandman is construed into an insult, and the capricious sprites mislead him on the first opportunity, and laugh heartily at his misadventures. They are great enemies of sluttery and encouragers of good husbandry. When not singing or dancing their chief nightly amusement is in riding the colts, and plaiting the manes, or tangling them with the seed-vessels of the burdock. Of a particular field in this neighbourhood it is reported that the farmer never puts his horses in it but he finds them in the morning in a state of great terror, panting and covered with foam. Their form of government is monarchical, as frequent mention is made of "the King of the piskies". We have a few stories of pisky changelings, the only proof of whose parentage is that "they did'nt goodey", (thrive). It would seem that fairy children of some age are entrusted to mortal care for a time, and again re-called to pisky-land. People are occasionally kidnapped by the little folk; hence an old nursery rhyme saith—

> "See saw; Margery Daw
> Sold her bed and lay upon straw;
> She sold her straw, and lay upon hay,
> Piskies came and carr'd her away".

A disposition to laughter is a striking trait in their character, and a person who laughs heartily and unrestrainedly is said to "laugh like a pisky". I have been able to gather little about the personality of these beings. My old friend, before mentioned, described them as about a span long, clad in green, and wearing straw hats, or little red caps, on their heads. Two only are known by name, and I have heard them addressed in the following rhyme:

> "Jack o' the lantern! Joan the wad,
> Who tickled the maid and made her mad;
> Light me home, the weather's bad".

I leave the stories of the piskey-led, of which we could furnish several modern instances, for the following ancient legends, all carefully copied from oral tradition.

Colman Grey.—A farmer, who formerly lived at Langreek, was returning one evening from a distant part of the farm, when, in crossing a particular field he saw to his surprise, sitting on a stone in the middle of it, a miserable looking little creature, human in appearance, though of diminutive size, and apparently starving with cold and hunger. Pitying its condition, and perhaps aware that it was of elfish origin, and that good luck would amply repay him for his kind treatment of it, he took it home, placed it by the warm hearth, and fed it with nice milk. The poor bantling soon recovered from the lumpish and only half sensible state in which it was found, and, though it never spoke, became very lively and playful. From the amusement which its strange tricks excited, it became a general favourite in the family, and the good folk really felt very sorry when it quitted them, which it did in a very unceremonious manner. After the lapse of three or four days, as the little fellow was gamboling about the farm kitchen, a shrill voice from the town-place or farm-yard was heard to call three times, "Colman Grey!" at which it sprang up, and gaining voice, cried, "Ho! Ho! Ho! my daddy is come!" flew through the key hole, and was never afterwards heard of.

A Voyage with the Piskies.—About a mile and a half to the east, on the shore of Talland bay, is the hamlet of Portallow, with its scattered farm houses, and the Green on which the children assemble at their sports. In old time, a lad in the employ of a farmer who occupied one of the homesteads, was sent to Polperro to procure some little household necessaries from the shop. Dark night had set in by the time he had reached Sand-hill, on his way home. When half way down the steep road, he heard a voice, "I'm for Portallow Green": As you are going my way, thought he, I may as well have your company; and he waited for a repetition of the sound. "I'm for Portallow Green" was soon repeated. "I'm for Portallow Green" answered the boy. Quick as thought he found himself on the Green, surrounded by a throng of little laughing piskies. They were scarcely settled before the cry was heard from several tiny voices, "I'm for Seaton Beach", (a fine expanse of sand between this place and Plymouth). Whether he was charmed by his brief taste of pisky society, or taken with their pleasant mode of travelling, is not stated; but instead of turning his pocket inside out, as many would have done, he immediately rejoined, "I'm for Seaton Beach". Off he was whisked, and in a moment found himself on Seaton Beach. After they had for a while "danced their ringlets to the whistling wind" the cry was changed to "I'm for the King of France's cellar"; and strange to say he offered no objection even to so long a journey. "I'm for the King of France's cellar" shouted the adventurous youth, as he dropped his parcel on the beach not far from the edge of the tide. Immediately he found himself in a spacious cellar, engaged with his mysterious companions in tasting the richest of wines. They then passed through grand rooms fitted up with a splendour which quite dazzled him. In one apartment the tables were covered with fine plate and rich viands, as if in expectation of a feast. Though in the main an honest lad, he could not resist a temptation to take away with him some memorial of his travels, and he pocketed one of the rich silver goblets which stood on the table. After a very short stay the word was raised, "I'm for Seaton Beach", which being repeated by the boy, he was taken back as quickly as he went and luckily reached the beach in time to save his parcel from the flowing tide. Their next destination was Portallow Green, where the piskies left our wondering traveller, who soon reached home, delivered his parcel, and received a compliment from the good wife for his dispatch. "You'd say so, if you only knowed where I've been" said he; "I've been with the piskies to Seaton Beach, and I've been to the King o' France's cellar; and all in five minutes". The boy's mazed" says the wife. "I thought you'd say I was mazed" answered the lad, "so I brought away this mug to show vor et", at the same time producing the goblet. The farmer and his family examined it, wondered at it, and ended by giving a full belief to the boy's strange story. The goblet is, unfortunately, not now to be shown for the satisfaction of those who may still doubt; but we are assured that it remained the property of the lad's family for generations after.

The Piskey Threshers.—The lext legend is connected with a particular farm-house in the neighbourhood, and well illustrates the capricious temper of the little folk, who are easily offended by an offer of reward, however delicately tendered.

Long, long ago, before threshing machines were invented, the farmer who lived at Colmans, on going to his barn one day was surprised at the extraordinary quantity of corn that had been threshed during the previous night, as well as puzzled to discover the mysterious agency by which it was effected. His curiosity led him to enquire into the matter; so at night, when the moon was up, he crept stealthily to the barn door, and, looking through a chink, saw a little fellow, clad in a very tattered suit of green, wielding the dreshel (flail) with astonishing vigour, and beating the floor with blows so rapid that the eye could not follow the motions of the implement. The farmer slunk away unperceived, and crept to bed, where he lay a long while awake thinking in what way he might best show his gratitude to the pisky for such an important service. He came to the conclusion at length, that, as the little fellow's clothes were old and ragged, the gift of a new suit would be a proper way to lessen the obligation, and accordingly, on the morrow he had a suit of green cloth made of what he judged to be the proper size, which he carried early in the evening to the barn, and left for the pisky's acceptance. At night the farmer stole to the door again to see how his gift was taken. He was just in time to see the elf put on the suit, which was no sooner done than looking down on himself admiringly, the little fellow sung—

> *"Pisky fine, and pisky gay,*
> *Pisky now will fly away".*

Or, according to other narrators—

> *"Pisky new coat, and pisky new hood,*
> *Pisky now will do no more good".*

From that time forward the farmer had no assistance from the fairy flail.

Another story tells how a farmer, looking through the key-hole, saw two elves threshing lustily, now and then interrupting their work to say to each other, in the smallest falsetto voice, "I tweat; you tweat?" The poor man, unable to contain his gratitude, incautiously thanked them through the key-hole, when the spirits who love to work "unheard and unespied", instantly vanished, and never after visited the barn.

They seem sometimes to have delighted in mischief for its own sake. Old Robin Hicks, who formerly lived in a house at "Quay Head", has more than once, on stormy winter nights, been alarmed at his supper by a voice sharp and shrill: "Robin! Robin! your boat is adrift". Loud was the laughter, and the *tacking* of hands, when they succeeded in luring Robin as far as the quay, where the boat was lying safely at her moorings.

The Fisherman and the Piskies.—John Taprail, long since dead, moored his boat one evening beside a barge of much larger size, in which

". . . managed to introduce his hat . . ."

small patch of moor that was visible; each snorting fire, and uttering a yelp of an indescribably frightful tone. No cottage, rock, or tree, was near to give the herdsman shelter, and nothing remained to him but to abandon himself to their fury, when a happy thought suggested a resource. Just as they were about to rush upon him, he fell on his knees in prayer. There was strange power in the holy words he uttered; for immediately, as if resistance had been offered, the hell-hounds stood at bay, howling more dismally than ever, and the hunter shouted "Bo shrove"! which, says my informant, means in the old language, the boy prays; at which they all drew off on some other pursuit and disappeared. This ghastly apparition loses much of its terrible character as we approach the more thickly populated districts, and our stories of the devil and his dandy dogs are very tame after this legend of the moors. Many of the tales which I have heard are so well attested, that there is some reason to conclude that the narrators have really seen a pack of fairies, (the local name, it is necessary to add, of the weasel), of which it is well known that they hunt gregariously at night-time, and, when so engaged, do not scruple to attack man.

Another object of superstition among our fishermen is the white hare, a being resembling the *letiche*. It frequents our quays by nights; and is quite harmless, except that its appearance is held to predict a storm.

8

POPULAR ANTIQUITIES—WITCHCRAFT, CHARMS, ETC.

I am sorry to say that here, though not in a greater degree than elsewhere in the West of England, that most degrading of all popular creeds, the belief in witchcraft, holds its ground very firmly; and of all superstitions, I fear, it will be the last to die out; since, to mention no other influence, the inductive process of reasoning will never be a popular one, and there will always be a greater number who, too impatient to question the material hastily resort to the spiritual for a ready explanation of all phenomena, down even to the creaking and oscillations of tables. Many strange coincidences are occurring daily, which, to minds not over nice about distinctions between *post* and *propter*, have all the relationship of cause and effect, and a supernatural origin is the readiest way of accounting for them, and the safest, because it cannot be successfully refuted. The notion that mysterious compacts are formed between evil spirits and wicked men has become nearly obsolete. In the present day, such a bargain is rarely suspected, and few are found hardy enough to avow themselves parties to so unholy a transaction. One instance has occurred within my remembrance of a poor unhappy, abandoned fellow who pretended, in vulgar parlance, to have sold himself to the devil, and was accordingly regarded by his neighbours as a miracle of impiety. He was not, however, actively vicious, never being known to use his supernatural powers of ill-doing, to the detriment of others, and only asked the foul fiend's assistance, when the depth of his potations had not left him enough to pay the reckoning. He was then accustomed to hold his hat up the chimney, and demand money, which was promptly showered down into it. The coin so obtained was always refused with a shudder, by the landlord, who was even glad to get quit of him on these terms. This compact with the spirit of evil is now but vaguely suspected as the secret of the witch's power.

The faculty of witchcraft is held to be hereditary, and it is not the least cruel of the effects of this horrible creed that many really good-natured souls have, on account of this supposed taint of blood, been kept aloof from their neighbours, and made miserable by being ever the object of unkind suspicions. When communications with such persons cannot be avoided, their ill-will is deprecated by a slavish deference. If met on the highway, care is taken to pass them on the right hand.

Witches are supposed to have the power of changing their shape, and resuming it again at will. A large hare, which haunted the neighbourhood, had on numberless occasions baffled the hounds, or carried off, unhurt, incredible quantities of shot. One luckless day it crossed the path of a party of determined sportsmen, who followed it for many weary miles, and fired several rounds with the usual want of success. Before

68

relinquishing the chase, one of them, who considered the animal as something beyond an ordinary hare, suggested the trial of silver bullets, and, accordingly, silver coins were beaten into slugs for the purpose. The hare was again seen, fired at, and this time wounded; though not so effectually as to prevent its running round the brow of the hill, and disappearing among the rocks. In searching for the hare they discovered instead, old Molly crouched under a shelving rock, panting and flushed by the long chase. From that day forward she had a limp in her gait.

The toad and the black cat are the most usual attendants of the witch, or rather the forms her imps most commonly assume. The appearance of a toad on the door-step is taken for a certain sign that the house is under evil influence, and the poor reptile is put to some frightfully barbarous death.

The most common results of the witch's malice, or, as it is termed, the *ill-wish*, are misfortunes in business, and diseases of an obstinate and deadly character in the family or among the cattle. The cow refuses "to give down her milk", the butter is spoilt in making, or the house is tormented by a visitation, in incredible numbers, of those insects said "to be familiar to man, and to signify love". There are a hundred other ways in which the evil influence may be manifested.

When witchcraft is suspected, the person *over-looked* has immediate recourse to the *conjurer*, the very bad representative of the astrologer of a former age. The *conjurer* is an important character in our country districts. He is resorted to by despairing lovers, he counsels those who are under the evil eye, and discloses the whereabouts of stolen goods. His answers, too, are given with true oracular ambiguity. "Own horn eat own corn", was his reply to a person who consulted him about the disappearance of various little household articles. A large endowment of natural wit, a small smattering of learning, and a slightly developed *morale* go to furnish out the conjurer. When he is appealed to in cases of suspected witchcraft, the certainty of weird influence is first proved beyond a doubt, and the first letter of the witch's name, or description of her person, is given, or even, (so it is said), her bodily presence shewn in a magic mirror. I know but little of the incantations practised on these occasions.

The certainty of the ill-wish being this established, and the person of the witch fixed on, the remembrance of some past "difference" or quarrel places the matter beyond doubt. This mode of proceeding to a conclusion is truly and quaintly described by old Dr. Harsenet:—

"Beware, look about you, my neighbours. If any of you have a sheep sick of the giddies, or a hog of the mumps, or a horse of the staggers, or a knavish boy of the school, or an idle girl of the wheel, or a young drab of the sullens, and hath not fat enough for her porrage, or butter enough for her bread, and she hath a little help of the epilepsy, or cramp, to teach her to roll her eyes, wry her mouth, gnash her teeth, startle with her body, hold her arms stiff, etc. . . . . And then when an old

Mother Nobs hath by chance called her 'idle young housewife', or bid the devil scratch her, then no doubt but Mother Nobs is the witch, and the young girl is owl-blasted".

One of the various methods of dissolving the spell is now resorted to. It is a belief that the power for evil ceases the moment blood is drawn from the witch, and this is now and then tried, as in a late instance when a man was summoned before the bench of magistrates, and fined for an offence of this kind. When an ox or other beast had died in consequence of the ill-wish, it is usual to take out the heart, stick it over with pins and nails, and roast it before the fire until the pins and nails have one by one dropped out of it, during which process the witch is supposed to be suffering in sympathy with the roasted heart. There are many stories told of how the wicked woman has been driven by these means to confess, and to loose the family from the spell. Recourse is sometimes had to measures of a less delicate description. When the friendly parasites become unpleasantly numerous, it was, not long since, the custom to send a friend, or even the town-crier, to shout near the door of the witch, "take back your flock!" "take back your flock!" a ceremony which was said to be followed by an abatement of the inconvenience.

The wiser method of prevention is very often taken, and the house and all it contains are protected from harm by the nailing of a horse-shoe over the doorway. There are few farm-houses without it, and scarcely a vessel or boat puts to sea without this talisman nailed to its mast or bowsprit. No evil spirit comes in its neighbourhood, and it renders all ill-wishes harmless to those who are under its guard. Another preventive of great fame is the *Care Tree* or Mountain Ash, of which more hereafter.

Besides the witch and the conjurer, we have yet another and a more pleasing character to mention, namely, the *charmer*. She is generally an elderly woman of good character and disposition and supposed to be gifted with supernatural power, which she exercises for good. By her incantations and ceremonies she staunches blood, cures inflamed eyes, and the erysipelas. I happed once on a manuscript account-book of a white witch or charmer, towards the end of which were, besides several material remedies, as "a drunch for a horse", and "a cure for the rumaticks", several charms and superstitious remedies. Risking the impropriety, I copied the following:—

A CHARM FOR THE BIT OF AN ADDER.

"Bradgty, bradgty, bradgty, under the ashing leaf. To be repeated three times, and strike your hand with the growing of the hare. Bradgty, bradgty, bradgty to be repeated three times before eight, eight before seven, and seven before six, and six before five, and five before four, and four before three, and three before two, and two before one, and one before every one, three times for the bit of an adder".

FOR A STRAIN.

"Christ rode over the bridge, Christ rode under the bridge; Vein to Vein; Strain to strain, I hope God will take it back againe".

70

FOR AGUE.

"When our Saviour saw the cross, whereon he was to be crucified, his body did shake. The Jews said, 'Hast thou an ague!' Our Saviour said, 'He that keepeth this in mind, thought, or writing, shall neither be troubled with ague or fever' ".

FOR THE TOOTHACHE.

"Peter sat at the gate of the Temple, and Christ said unto him 'What aileth thee?' he said, 'Oh, my tooth!' Christ said unto Peter, follow me, and thou shalt not feel the tooth ache no more. To be hung round, or about the patient's neck".

FOR CRAMP.

"The cramp is keenless, Mary was sinless: when Mary bore Jesus, let the cramp go away in the name of Jesus".

FOR WILDFIRE.

"Christ he walketh over the land, Carried the wildfire in his hand, He rebuked the fire and bid it stand; Stand, wildfire, stand, (three times repeated). In the name of the Father, Son, and Holy Ghost".

FOR A BURN.

"As I passed over the river Jordan, I met with Christ, and he says unto me, 'Woman, what aileth thee?' 'Oh! Lord my flesh doth burn'. The Lord saith unto me, 'Two angels cometh from the west, one for fire, one for frost, out fire and in frost, in the name of, &c.

FOR SCAL.

"There was three angels cam from the West
The wan brought fiar, and the other brought frost.
And the other brought the book of Jesus Christ
In the name of the Father &c."

FOR STANCHING BLOOD.

'Our Saviour was born of Bethleam of Judeah. As He passed by revoor of Jorden, the waters waid were all in one. The Lord ris up his holy hand. and bid the waters still to stan, and so shall the blood. Three times".

A CHARM FOR BLOOD.

"Baptized in the river Jordan, when the water was wild, the water was good, the water stood, so shall thy blood. In the name &c."

FOR A THORN.

"Jesus walked upon the earth, he pricked his foot with a thorn, his blood sprang up to heaven, his flesh never rankled nor perished, no more shall not thine. In the name, &c.

ALSO,

"When Christ was upon middle earth the Jews pricked him, his blood spring up into heaven, his flesh never rotted nor fustered, no more I hope will not thine. In the name, &c.

ALSO,

"Our Saviour was fastened to the Cross with nails and thorns, which neither rats nor rankles, no more shan't thy finger. (For a thorn three times).

TO CURE WORTS.

"Take a nat *of a reed, and strike the wort downwards three times, berey the reed".*

Before closing this chapter, I would say, for the sake of the less instructed of my fellow townsmen, the dark side of whose character I have, it is to be feared, been here disclosing, that superstition does not necessarily imply ignorance, in the ordinary sense of that term. Though superstitious, they are, with regard to the realities of life, as shrewd and sagacious as their neighbours.

9

POPULAR ANTIQUITIES—FASTS AND FESTIVALS

Of Polperro it may be said, in the words of Herrick,

> "*For sports and pagentries and plays,*
> *Thou hast thy eyes and holidays;*"

and of these I proceed to give some account.

New Year's Day is the time of mutual congratulation; the interchange of good wishes, and more substantial evidences of friendship. The character of the coming twelve months, for good or bad fortune, is foretold by the appearance of things on the morning of the new year. A trivial mishap, or the slightest instance of good luck, has now more than its usual significance, inasmuch as it predicts, in a general way, the course of events through the coming year.

Valentine's Day has no local peculiarity worth noticing.

Hall Monday—Nicky-nan Night.—The reports of the Royal Institution of Cornwall (1842), contain the following notice of the strange customs which distinguish this day:—

"*On the day termed 'Hall' Monday, which precedes Shrove Tuesday, about dusk of the evening it is the custom for boys, and, in some cases, for those above the age of boys, to prowl about the streets with short clubs, and to knock loudly at every door, running off to escape detection on the slightest sign of a motion within. If, however, no attention be excited, and especially if any article be discovered negligently exposed, or carelessly guarded, then the things are carried away; and on the following morning are seen displayed in some conspicuous place to expose the disgraceful want of vigilance supposed to characterise the owner. The time when this is practised is called* Nicky-nan-night; *and the individuals concerned are supposed to represent some imps of darkness, that seize on, and expose unguarded moments*".

Further on this custom is compared with a somewhat similar one in Brittany, known as Ninc-kyn-nan-neuf; and a connexion is sought between the mischievous imp and our harvest *neck*, of which we shall presently hear. To this account of a festival which I have often assisted in celebrating, I may add that on the following eve, (Shrove Tuesday), the clubs were again in requisition; but on this occasion the blows on the door were in time to the following chant—

> "*Nicky nicky nan,*
> *Give me some pancake, and then I'll be gone.*
> *But if you give me none*
> *I'll throw a great stone,*
> *And down your door shall come*".

Heath, in his account of the Scilly Islands, described a similar custom, which, he says, is used also in Spain as well as in Cornwall. In Mr. Hugh Miller's delightful volume on the traditiony lore of Cromarty, mention is made of an observance too much like our own not to have had the same origin.

"*After night-fall the young fellows of the town formed themselves into parties, of ten or a dozen, and, breaking into the gardens of the graver of the inhabitants, stole the best and heaviest of their cabbages: converting these into bludgeons by stripping off the lower leaves; they next scoured the streets and lanes, thumping at every door as they passed, until their uncouth weapons were beaten to pieces. When disarmed in this way, all the parties united into one, and providing themselves with a cart, drove it before them with the rapidity of a chaise-and-four through the principal streets*".

Lent.—An old custom, now quite defunct, was observed here not long since in the beginning of Lent. A figure made up of straw and cast-off clothes was drawn or carried round the town, amid much noise and merriment, after which it was either burnt, shot at, or brought to some other ignominious end. This image was called "Jack o' Lent", and was, doubtless, intended to represent Judas Iscariot. A dirty slovenly fellow is often termed a "Jack o' Lent".

Palm Sunday.—The observance of Palm Sunday is almost discontinued. The substitute for palms is the catkins of the willow, locally termed "cats and dogs". It was until lately the custom to allow parish 'prentices a holiday on this day, that they might visit their parents or friends.

April 1st is April Fool's Day here as elsewhere.

Good Friday brings a holiday and hot-cross-buns. It is the custom for the farm labourers inland to make a journey to the sea-coast on this day, to pick "wrinkles". In some of our farm-houses the Good-Friday bun may be seen hanging by a string to the bacon-rack; slowly diminishing until the return of the season replaces it by a fresh one. It is of sovereign good in all manner of diseases afflicting the family or the cattle. I have more than once seen a little of this cake grated into a warm mash for a sick cow.

Easter Day.—A holiday. The elderly folk speak of their rising early on the morning of this day to see the sun dance.

May 1st—Dipping Day.—Our May-day customs require a fuller description, as they seem to be peculiar. There is little in the many accounts of this famous festival as observed in various parts of England, which resembles our mode of keeping it. I cannot learn from our oldest people that the May-pole has been of late years erected in Polperro, though within my memory it has been seen in the churchtown of Pelynt. There are, however, other remarkable sports which are kept up with unabated vigour to this day. On May morning the children, and even adults, go out into the country, and fetch home branches of the narrow-leaved elm, or flowering boughs of the white-thorn, both of which are called "May". At a later hour all the boys of the village sally forth with bucket, can, or other vessel, and avail themselves of a licence which the season confers, to "dip", or well-nigh drown, without regard to person or circumstance, the passenger who has not the protection of a piece of "may", conspicuously stuck in his dress, at the same time that they sing, "the first of May is dipping day". The sprig of elm, or hawthorn, is, I suppose, held to be a proof that the bearer has not failed to rise early "to do observance to a morn of May". There is a great deal of fun on the occasion, for many an unfortunate body who has failed to comply with an ancient custom is seen slinking home like a drowned rat. This manner of keeping May-day is, I have heard, common in Cornwall. We are now favoured with a call from the boy with his pretty garland, gay with bright flowers, and gaudily painted bird's eggs, who expects some little gratuity for the sight.

It would seem that the white-thorn is, not here only, the especial plant of May; but inasmuch as it is a very rare occurrence to find it in flower by the modern May-day, it is convenient to have another substitute in the boughs of the narrow-leaved elm, which have just then burst into full leaf.

The May-pole, as I have said, has been seen very lately in the neighbourhood; but this, the better known portion of the May ceremonial, has quite died out among us. It has been a question how far it were possible, if desirable, to restore a picturesque old custom, rendered dear to us by the description of a hundred poets, before the memory of it is quite lost by the peasantry. My own impression is, that it is not possible. A marked change has taken place in the relationship between the squire and his tenantry: the feudal devotedness of the latter has given place to a feeling more of respect than love; and the benevolence of the former, which was never more active than at present, is directed to other and more worthy ends than formerly. The school-feast, the ploughing-match, and the horticultural show, have driven out May-poles and Christmas misrule. Whereas in former days the country gentleman thought a day's merriment cheaply purchased at the price of a sapling from his broad plantations, and a small present to help trick out Friar Tuck and Maid Marian, the people can now only obtain their May-pole surreptitiously. This goes far to explain the decline and fall of the old English merry-making, at least, as far as concerns this neighbourhood. Old things give place to new, and, as the poet says of the grand old days of Arthur and his knights, so we may, in less degree, say of the old May-day:—

"*Nature brings not back the mastodon*
Nor we those times".

Whitsuntide.—A holiday chiefly remarkable for a custom still kept up by children of going to some farm-house in the country to partake of milk and cream. The old usage of collecting for Whitsun ales has quite gone out.

Midsummer Day.—What Hallowe'en is to the Scotch, this day is to us; the season of love divination. The youth of both sexes but especially, say some, the girls meet; those who have sweethearts to determine whether they are constant, and those whose choice is yet unfixed, to enquire whom they are fated to marry. There are many methods of consulting the future practised on this day. Some of the oracles are consulted plainly; others require many preparatory ceremonies. Sometimes the *actual* presence of the wished-for lover is manifested, at other times the answer is vouchsafed by dreams. I subjoin a few of the forms of divination for the use of those who may need them.

On Midsummer morning get up early and go into the woods and fields in search of one of those rarities, an even-leaved ash, or clover. If so lucky as to find it, carry it about you; as an old couplet assures you that with

> *"Even-leaved ash or four-leaved clover,*
> *You'll meet your true love before the day's over".*

Get a glass of water, and having broken an egg, and separated the white from the yolk, throw the former into it, and place it in the sunshine. You will soon see, with a little aid from your fancy, the ropes and yards of a vessel, if you husband is to be a sailor, or plough and team, if he is to be a farmer.

Borrow a wedding-ring, and suspend it *steadily* in a tall wine-glass by a hair taken from your own head. Think on your sweetheart, if you desire to be assured of his constancy; or on the one you desire for a lover; and if the fates are propitious, the ring will strike against the sides of the glass.

The Bible and key is another method, used both for this purpose, and also for the detection of a thief.

Get some hemp seed, take it into the garden at midnight, and scattering it, repeat these words,—

> *"Hemp seed I sow, hemp seed I hoe,*
> *In hopes that my true love will come after me and mow".*

You will then see the apparition of your future lover with a scythe, in the act of mowing.

Spread bread and cheese on the table and sit down to it alone, observing strict silence. As the clock strikes the hour of midnight, your future lover will join you at supper.

Get a piece of wedding-cake, and carry it upstairs backwards; tie it in your left stocking, with your right garter, and place it under your pillow. Get into bed backwards, keeping strict silence all the while, and your dreams will reveal to you your predestined sweetheart. These "ceremonies due" must be done aright, or the divination fails.

St. Peter's Day. Peter's-tide.—The patron saint of Polperro, as has been said, is St. Peter, to whom a little chapel built on the Seaward-hill, (still called Chapel Hill), was dedicated. His festival is kept on the tenth of July. Here it may be remarked that the Polperro people never wholly complied with the change of style which was effected in the year 1751, and which had, to the popular mind, the effect of sponging out eleven days of their life. It seems to have been as unpopular here as elsewhere, and even now has only been partially accepted, for we have *new* and *old* Christmas day, while the old St. Peter's day is retained. At Peter's-tide is our annual feast or fair. Though a feeble and insignificant matter, it is still, with the young, the great event of the year. Long may it continue; for notwithstanding the few secenes of riot and disorder which it sees, it gathers round the parental board each year, those whom the cares of the world have compelled to separate, and is, indeed, an annual rogation day for renewing the old landmarks of affection. It is also worthy of notice as being marked by a strange medley of old usages, some of very ancient derivation, but modified by a succession of altering circumstances.

On the eve of the fair is the prefatory ceremony of a bonfire. The young fishermen go from house to house and beg money to defray the expenses. At night-fall a large pile of faggots and tar-barrels is built on the beach, and amid the cheers of a congregated crowd of men, women, and children, (for it is a favour never denied to children to stay up and see the bonfire), the pile is lighted. The fire blazes up, and men and boys dance merrily round it, and keep up the sport till the fire burns low enough, then they venturously leap through the flames. It is a most animated scene; the whole valley lit up by the bright red glow, bringing into strong relief front and gable of picturesque old houses, each window crowded with eager and delighted faces; while around the fire is a crowd of ruddy lookers-on, shutting in a circle of impish figures leaping like salamanders through the flames.

This fire was, no doubt, originally intended to celebrate the great solstitial feast, but was in later times, deferred until the festival of St. Peter. The very system which places particular spots under the patronage of certain saints, is but a modification of a pagan usage. The Bacchanalia and Floralia are still observed, but the heathen gods and goddesses are metamorphosed into saints and martyrs.

We are too apt to speak of our old popular beliefs and usages as having been introduced by late immigrants; but though this may in a great number of instances be true, yet a large number of them may be considered, with much probability, of far older date. The worship of Baal or the Deified Sun, the chief source of light and heat, and the most striking of all the great agencies which influence animal and vegetable life, must have been the earliest and most widely spread of all idolatries: and to the present day it exists in its integrity, or survives in popular customs, all over Europe and Asia, as well as in parts of Africa. We are taught, however, to consider this worship to have been introduced into Britain by Phoenician traders, and with reason, considering that Baal was their principal deity. So wonderfully has this old heathen rite been preserved, that the account of the custom observed by the Hindoos at the present day, might serve with a few alterations for a description of our own *Bealtine*, as observed in some parts of England, Scotland, and more especially Ireland.

The next day the fair begins, a trivial matter except to the children who are dressed in their Sunday clothes, and to the village girls in their best gowns and gaudiest ribbons. Stalls, or "standings", laden with fairings, sweetmeats, and toys, line the lower part of Lansallos-street, near the strand. There are, besides, strolling Thespians; fellows who draw unwary youth into games or hazard, where the risk is mainly on one side; ballad singers; *penny-peep* men, who show and describe to wondering boys the most horrid scenes of the latest murder; jugglers and tumblers also display their skill. In the neighbouring inn the fiddler plays his liveliest tunes at two-pence the reel, which the swains gallantly pay. The first day of the fair is merely introductory, for the excitement is rarely allayed under three; and it may be doubted if the equilibrium of Polperro is quite steadied until the end of the week. The second day is much livelier than the first, and has for its great event the wrestling match on the Strand, or perhaps a boat race. On the third day we have the mayor-choosing, never a valid ceremony, but a broad burlesque. The person who is chosen to this post of mimic dignity is generally some half-witted, or drunken fellow who, tricked out in tinsel finery, elects his staff of constables, and these, armed with staves, accompany his chariot, (some jowter's cart dressed with green boughs), through the town, stopping at each inn, where he makes a speech full of large promises to his listeners of full work, better wages, and a liberal allowance of beer during his year of mayoralty. He then demands a quart of the landlord's ale, which is gauged with mock ceremony, and if adjudged short of measure is, after being emptied, broken on the wheel of the car. Having completed the perambulation of the town, his attendants often made some facetious end of the pageant by wheeling the mayor in his chariot with some impetus into the tide, where, if his deep potations have not dimmed his power of reflection, he has time to think on the uncertainty of earthly dignity, and the fickleness of popular favour, failings which have been bewailed by greater men.

The fair is losing even its small importance year by year, and may soon dwindle to nothing; but, the small revelling and misrule notwithstanding, it will leave many things to be regretted.

> *"Happy" people "best content*
> *With the cheapest merriment,*
> *And possess no other feare*
> *Than to want the wake next yeare".*

Harvest.—This season has a few peculiar customs well worthy of notice. Towards the end of harvest when the last few stalks of the wheat-crop fall before the scythe, they are seized by the man who cuts them, and borne home in triumph. They are then woven into a miniature sheaf with projecting arms, and bedecked with daisies and other flowers to form the *neck* or *nick*. In the evening the *neck* is taken to the mowhay by one of the harvest-men, who proceeds to a good distance from the others, and on an elevated spot proclaims in his loudest voice, "I have him! I have him! I have him!" One from the company enquires as loudly, "What have'e?" three times. "*A neck! a neck! a neck!*" replies the first, and the assembled harvesters send up three loud hurrahs. The *neck* is taken in, and hung to the beam in the farm kitchen, where, in some cases, it remains until the next year supplants it by a new one, or is more commonly given on Christmas day to the master ox in the stall, whose perquisite it is.

A somewhat similar custom used to be observed on finishing the barley-mow. The man whose lot it was to place the terminal or *crow-sheaf* on the mow, held it up aloft, shouting three times, "I have him!" and a ceremony like that just described was gone through, with the only substitution of a *crow* for a *neck*. In the course of an evening's walk in latter harvest, the sound of these merry shouts, mellowed by distance, is a joyous accompaniment to the other rural delights of this pleasant season.

In many parts of England it is the custom to form the last handful from the reaper's hook into some resemblance of a human figure, which is brought home from the field with much merriment. This *Kern-baby*, *Harvest-maiden*, *Ivy-girl*, as it is variously termed, has been thought to represent Ceres; but, according to our own country-folk, a very few of whom retain even a vague notion of its meaning, the *neck* would seem to be the representation of some mischievous, rather than beneficent Deity. One is tempted to trace a connection between our *Nick*, and the Scandinavian *Neck* or *Nikkar*, a sort of Kelpie or water-spirit of mischievous if not savage propensities. This is plausible when we try to explain our Hall-Monday ceremony, but not so satisfactory in the illustration of the harvest observances.

This sweet season to which the labours and cares of the farmer have been long hopefully directed, and when the promises of the year are to end in fulfilment, has generally been a time of rejoicing and gratitude; but the harvest dinners of Carew's time are nearly gone out, with their merriment and riot.

Ringing-night is on the fourth of November, the eve of Gunpowder plot. The usual belfry rules, imposing fines on those who in a drunken or "choleric mood" should overturn a bell or "by unskilful handling mar a peal" are, for the time, not rigidly enforced, and I fear that many cracked bells can date their ruin from this night.

Christmas comes next, a time of genial mirth and heartiness, when general social regulations are by common consent relaxed. Misrule has happily gone out, and is replaced by soberer, but still noisy jollity. The time is notified by the evergreens with which every window is garnished. Poor old women now "go a gooding", travelling the parish over to collect from their richer neighbours the measure of flour for the cake, made yellow with saffron and besprinkled with currants; or the Christmas pudding. On Christmas-eve the mirth begins, when the *mock* or yule-log is lighted, it may be, from a portion saved from the last year's fire. In farm-houses the husbandmen and neighbours come in about evening and spend some hours in singing carols, clearing their voices by occasional draughts of cider. The travelling hawker has been round with his penny broadsheet, where "The first good joy our Mary had;" "As I sat on a sunny bank;" and "God rest ye merry gentlemen," are in company with "As shepherds watched their flocks by night;" Kirke White's "Star of Bethlehem;" and others which seem out of place in such almost ludicrous company. The provincial Catnach has illustrated the sheet at top by the "Flight into Egypt" and other similar scenes.

In town the family, flocking round the *mock*, are interrupted by the cheerfully tolerated intrusion of the goosey-dancers. The boys and girls rifle their parents' wardrobe of old gowns and coats, and disguise themselves, their mien, and speech, so cleverly that it is impossible to identify them. They are allowed, and are not slow to take, the large amount of licence which the season warrants; for it is considered a mark of a churlish disposition to take offence at anything they do or say. Accordingly they enter without ceremony; dance, sing and carry on an extemporaneous dialogue well spiced with native wit. After testing, unasked perhaps, whatever may be on the table, they beg money to make merry with. The children are much amused, and the mumners leave with a benediction.

" 'Twas as good as a Christmas play", is still our best comparison for anything that is funny, though this entertainment has for nearly half a century been discontinued. It may have been a remnant of the *guary-mirkl*, or miracle play, which in remote times was performed in the *round* or amphitheatre to amuse our Celtic forefathers; the latter dramas however have not been like the earlier ones, on Scripture subjects, but based on later romance. The last one I have intelligence of represented the achievements of George, and his victory over the Dragon. The theatre was a long room over some fish-cellar, or the largest chamber of the inn, and the players were the boys and girls of the town. A subscription had been previously made for the purchase of "properties", and the services of the damsels had been volunteered in arranging the costumes and other adornments. The play opened with the entrance of a page, who, after a brief speech, introduced a white-haired, tottering old man, yet having a mirthful eye and ruddy face, who announced himself thus:

> "*Here come I, old Father Christmas,*
> *Welcome, or welcome not,*
> *I hope old Father Christmas*
> *Will never be forgot*".

After improvising some fun, he went out, to be followed by the Turkish knight, breathing loud words of defiance against St. George. The armed saint suddenly appeared upon the stage and recounted his exploits:

> "*with my sword and spear*
> *I won three crowns of gold.*
> *I fought the dragon bold,*
> *And brought him to the slaughter,*
> *By that I gained fair Sabra,*
> *The King of Egypt's daughter*".

They fought and the Turkish Knight fell. St. George, with the humanity which should accompany bravery, called for a doctor to heal this "deep and deadly wound". A doctor came, and by the aid of a little

"Elicumpane" raised the Turkish Knight for a time but only to fall finally before the onslaught of St. George. A hobby-horse trotted in and removed the dead body. A bold dragon who had infested the country was next defied by the Saint, who was not daunted by the entrance of the dreadful monster, although he threatened,

"With my long teeth and scurvy jaw
I'll seize thee up within my maw".

The dragon was then valiantly encountered by the knight, and, after some struggles, slain. This part of the dragon was not played without some danger, for, it being necessary that he breathe forth sulphurous flames, accomplished by putting a squib in his snout, the explosive compound was sometimes thrown inward by the incautious elevation of the monstrous snout, to the damage of the player. A little bye-play followed, and St. George wound up the drama with

"Gentlemen and ladies! the sport is almost ended;
Come pay to the box, it is highly commended.
The box it would speak if it had but a tongue,
Come throw in your money, and think it no wrong".

This was "very tragical mirth", but, as Theseus said, "the worst are no worse if imagination amend them".

On Christmas Eve, at midnight, the cattle are said to observe the time by falling on their knees in the stall.

Inoccent's Day, Dec. 28th.—Our housewifes always refrain from washing clothes, and from scrubbing and cleaning generally, on this day.

Among the superstitions marking particular months and days are the following:

It is unlucky to buy a broom in May.

"A warm May makes a fat church-hay".
"When Easter falls in Lady-day's lap
Beware old England of a clap".

Friday is an unlucky day for the commencement of any work or enterprise.

"Saturday's moon, if it comes once in seven years it comes too soon".

The days of the week are thus supposed to indicate the destinies of children:

"Sunday's child is full of grace,
Monday's child is fair in face,
Tuesday's child is full of woe,
Wednesday's child has far to go,
Thursday's child is inclined to thieving,
Friday's child is free in giving,
Saturday's child works hard for his living".

10

POPULAR ANTIQUITIES—SCRAPS OF FOLK-LORE

There are numerous disjointed fragments of folk-lore which have been so sadly mis-shapen by time as to defy all attempt to classify them, and yet are worthy of being preserved. These are the superstitions connected with animals, plants, and things inanimate; and the medical or other virtues attributed to them.

The domestic treatment of disease among our poor consists, as we have seen, chiefly of charms and ceremonies. In many cases also we may notice remnants of old medical creeds, such as the doctrine of signatures, and the notion of sympathies and antipathies between separate and dissimilar bodies. In the cure for haemorrhage, for instance, the preference is shown to medicines of a bright-red colour; in nettle-rash a decoction of nettles is given; and to patients sickening of any other rashes, saffron tea, the brightest coloured liquid known, is administered. The fisherman whose hand has been pierced by a hook is very careful to preserve the hook from rust during the healing of the wound. The following instances will illustrate the superstitious character of the household medicine of the poorer of our country-people.

If an infant is suffering from the thrush, it is taken, fasting, on three following mornings, to have its mouth blown into by "a person who never knew his father"; that is to say, a posthumous child. If afflicted with the whooping-cough, it is fed with the bread and butter of a family, the heads of which bear the names of John and Joan—a serious thing for the poor couple in time of an epidemic; or if a piebald horse is to be found in the country, the child is taken to it, and passed thrice under its belly; the mere possession of such a beast conferring the power of curing this disease. The owner of a piebald horse stated that he has frequently been stopped on the road by anxious mothers who enquired of him in a casual way, what was good for the whopping cough; and the thing he mentioned, however inappropriate or absurd, was held to be a certain remedy in that particular case.

The passing of children through holes in the earth, rocks, or trees, once an established rite, is still practised in various parts of Cornwall. With us, boils are cured by creeping on the hands and knees beneath a bramble which has grown into the soil at both ends. Children affected with hernia, are still passed through a slit in an ash sapling before sunrise, fasting; after which the slit portions are bound up; and as they unite, so the malady is cured. The ash is indeed a tree of many virtues; venomous reptiles are never known to rest under its shadow, and a single blow from an ash-stick is instant death to an adder. Struck by the bough of any other tree, the reptile is said to retain marks of life until the sun goes down. The antipathy of the serpent to the ash is a very old and popular belief.

The mountain-ash, or *care*, has still greater repute among our country folk in the curing of ills arising from supernatural as well as ordinary causes. It is dreaded by evil spirits; renders null the spell of the witch; and had many other wonderful properties. The countryman will carry for years a piece of wood in his pocket as a charm against the ill-wish, or as a remedy for his rheumatism. If his cow is out of health, and he suspects her to be overlooked, away he runs to the nearest wood and brings home branches of "care," which he suspends over her stall, and wreathes round her horns; after which he considers her safe.

Boys, when stung by nettles, have great faith in the antidotal properties of the dock; and, whilst rubbing it into the part in pain, repeat: "Out nettle, in dock,—nettle, nettle, stung me".

The cures for warts are many and various. A piece of flesh is taken secretly, and rubbed over the warts; it is then buried; and as the flesh decays, the warts vanish; or some mysterious vagrant asks to have them carfully counted, and marking the number on the inside of his hat, leaves the neighbourhood, when the warts also disappear.

There are some animals the subject of superstitious veneration, and a much greater number whose actions are supposed to convey intimations of the future.

The howling of dogs; the continual croaking of ravens over a house; and the ticking of the death-watch; portend death. The magpie is bird of good or ill-omen, according to the number seen at a time:

"One for sorrow; two for mirth;
Three for a wedding; four for a birth".

A crowing hen is a bird of ill-luck; for an old proverb in use here says: "A whistling woman and a crowing hen, are two of the unluckiest things under the sun". The first is always reproved, and the latter got rid of without loss of time.

If on the first hearing of the cuckoo, the sounds proceed from the right hand, it signifies that you will be prosperous; or to use the launguage of my informant, a country lad: "You will go vore in the world"; if from the left, ill-luck is before you. Children are frequently heard to hail the cuckoo in verse as follows:

"The cuckoo is a fine bird,
He sings as he flies,
He brings us good tidings,
He tells us no lies.
He sucks the sweet flowers
To make his voice clear,
And when he sings "Cuckoo"
The summer draws near".

Particular honour is paid to the robin and the wren. A local distich says:

"He that hurts a robin or a wren
Will never prosper sea or land".

83

This gives than a protection which the most mischievous urchin rarely dares to violate.

It is a very prevalent belief that a bed-pillow stuffed with the feathers of wild birds renders the departure of the dying painful and prolonged. Death is also thought to be delayed until the ebb of the tide.

The killing of the first adder you see predicts that you will triumph over you enemies; the slough of an adder hung on the rafters preserves the house against fire.

Our forefathers appear to have been amongst those who considered bees as possessing a portion "divinae mentis"; for there is a degree of deference yet paid to them which would scarcely be offered to beings endowed with only ordinary animal instinct. On the death of a relative, the bees are made acquainted with the event by the moving of the hive, and putting it in mourning by a piece of black cloth or crape tied on it. If this is neglected, they are said to forsake the hive. The sale of bees is a very unlucky proceeding, and they are generally transferred to another owner with the silent understanding that a bushell of wheat, (the constant equivalent of a swarm), is expected in exchange. When death happens in a family, the indoor plants are likewise put in mourning; this omitted, they soon droop and die.

The cricket is a bringer of good luck, and its departure from a house is a sign of coming misfortune.

Amongst the omens believed in, or existing in proverbs, I may further mention, thet the breaking of a looking-glass entails "seven years' trouble, but no want"; that the dirgeful singing of children portends a funeral. There is scarcely a sensation but has its meaning. If the left palm itches, you will have to pay money; if the right, to receive. If the sole of your foot itches, you will walk over strange ground; if the knee, kneel in a strange church; if the elbow, you will sleep with a strange bed-fellow; if your ear tingles, you will hear sudden news. If you shiver, someone is walking over the spot where your grave is to be. If the cheek burns, some one is talking scandal of you. I have often heard the lines spoken:

> "Right cheek! left cheek! why do you burn?
> Cursed be she that doth me any harm:
> If she be a maid, let her be staid;
> If she be a widow, long let her mourn;
> But if it be my own true love—burn, cheek, burn!"

Even those white patches so common on the nails are not without their significance. They are called *gifts*, and it is said that

> "A gift on the thumb is sure to come,
> A gift on the finger is sure to linger".

In offering such scraps as these, I have been half inclined to excuse myself with Carew, and say: "If I become blameworthy in speaking of such toyes, Scipio and Lelius shall serve for my patrons, who held it no shame to spend time in their gathering". These bits are of some *general* value however, not being the product of *local* fancy, but believed in over a wide geographical range; and therefore not without some worth to the generaliser who, with materials collected by other observers, may hereafter shape them all into a consistent whole.

FIRST SEA-CHART OF CORNWALL

By J. WAGHENAER, 1584

Just published. A facsimile copy of the first sea-chart of Cornwall. It was made by the Dutch cartographer, J. WAGHENAER in 1584. The original is very rare. It is a highly decorative map with elaborate cartouches, compasses, ships, and sea monsters. It shows the harbours of Cornwall in the 16th century. Size 20 x 13 inches. Only 200 copies issued.

HAND COLOURED

PRICE 30/-

From V. Graham, 6 Queen's Terrace, Newcastle upon Tyne, 2.

11

Jonathan Couch's History of Polperro was published posthumously and his editor Thomas Q. Couch added a number of extra notes at the end. Among them is the following story:

Many years ago I listened to the recital of the following Talland legend by a country fire-side, and immediately exercised myself in putting it into shape without in any material particular altering it.

THE SPECTRAL COACH

"You have heard of such a spirit, and well you know
The superstitious, idle-headed eld
Received and did deliver to our age
This tale of Herne the Hunter for a truth."

The old vicarage-house at Talland, as seen from the Looe road; its low roof and grey walls peeping prettily from between the dense boughs of ash and elm that environed it; was as picturesque an object as you could wish to see. The seclusion of its situation was enhanced by the character of the house itself. It was an odd-looking, old-fashioned building, erected apparently in an age when asceticism and self-denial were more in vogue than at present, with a stern disregard of the comfort of the inhabitant, and in utter ignorance or contempt of received principles of taste. As if not secure enough in its retirement, a high wall enclosing a courtlage in front, effectually protected its inmates from the passing wayfarer, and only revealed the upper part of the house, with its small gothic windows, slated roofs, and heavy chimneys, partly hidden by the evergreen shrubs which grew in the enclosure. Such was it until its removal a few years since, and such was it as it lay sweetly in the shadows of an autumnal evening one hundred and thirty years ago, when a stranger in the garb of a country labourer knocked at the wicket gate which conducted to the court. After a little delay a servant-girl appeared, and finding that the countryman bore a message to the vicar, admitted him within the walls, and conducted him along a paved passage to the little, low, damp parlour where sat the good man. The Rev. Mr. Dodge, to whom the messenger was thus introduced, was in many respects a remarkable man, and you would instantly have judged as much of him as he sat before the fire in his high-back chair in an attitude of thought, arranging, perhaps, the heads of his next sabbath's discourse. His heavy eyebrows, throwing into shade his serious eyes, and, indeed the whole contour of his face marked him as a man of great firmness of character, and of much moral and personal courage. His suit of sober black, and full bottomed periwig also added to his dignity, and gave him an appearance of greater age than he was entitled to, for he was then only verging on sixty. The time and the place gave him abundant exercise for his valour and decision, for many of his parishioners got their living by the contraband trade, and were too often men of great daring, and very unscrupulous; little likely to bear with patience reflections on the dishonesty of their calling. Nevertheless the vicar was fearless in reprehending it, and his frank exhortations were at least quietly listened to on account of the simple honesty of the man, and his well-known kindness of heart. The eccentricity of his life, too, had a wonderful effect in procuring him the respect, not to say the awe of a superstitious race. Ghosts in those day had more freedom accorded them, or had more business with the visible world than at present; and the parson was frequently required by his parishioners to draw from the uneasy spirit the dread secret which troubled it, or by the aid of the solemn prayers of the church to set it at rest for ever. Our parson had a fame as an exorcist which was not confined to the bounds of his parish, nor limited to the age in which he lived.

"Well, my good man, what brings you hither?" said the clergyman to the messenger.

"A letter, please your reverence, from Mr. Grylls of Lanreath", answered the countryman, handing him a letter.

Mr. Dodge opened it, and read as follows:—

'MY DEAR BROTHER DODGE,

I have ventured to trouble you, at the earnest request of the people of my parish, with a matter of which some particulars have, doubtless, reached you, and which has caused, and is causing much terror in my neighbourhood. For its fuller explication, I will be so tedious as to recount to you the whole of this strange story as it has reached my ears, for as yet I have not satisfied my eyes of its truth. It has been told me by men of honest and good report, (witnesses of what they relate), with such strong assurances, that it behoves us to look more closely into the matter. There is in this neighbourhood a barren bit of moor which had no owner, or rather more than one, for the lords of the adjoining manors debated its ownership between themselves, and both determined to take it from the poor, who have, time without mind, regarded it as common. And truly it is little to the credit of these gentlemen, that they should strive for a thing so worthless as scarce to bear the cost of law, and yet of no mean value to poor labouring people. The two litigants, however, contested it with as much violence as if it had been a field of great price and especially one, an old man, whose thoughts should have been less set on possessions he was soon to leave, had so set his heart on the success of his suit, that the loss of it a few years back is said to have much hastened his death. Nor, indeed, after death, if current reports are worthy of credit, does he quit his claim to it; for at night-time his apparition is seen on the moor to the great fright of the neighbouring villagers. A public path leads by at no great distance from the spot, and on divers occasions has the labourer returning from his work been scared nigh unto lunacy by sights and sounds of a very dreadful character. The appearance is said to be that of a man habited in black, driving a carriage drawn by headless horses. This is, I avow, very marvellous to believe, but it has had so much credible testimony tn my parish that some steps seem necessary to allay the excitement it causes. I have been applied to for this purpose, and my present business is to ask your assistance in

*the matter, either io quiet the minds of the country people if it be only
a simple terror; or if there be truth in it, to set the troubled spirit of the man
at rest. My messenger who is a hard-working, trustworthy man, will give
you more information if it be needed, for, from report he is acquainted
with most of the circumstances, and will bring back your advice, and, I
trust, promise of assistance.*

*Not doubting of your help herein, I do with my very hearty commenda-
tion commit you to God's protection and blessing, and am,*

Your very loving Brother,

R. GRYLLS."

This remarkable letter was read and re-read while the countryman
sat watching its effect on the parson's countenance, in surprise that it
changed but little from its usual sedate and settled character. Turning
at length to the man, Mr. Dodge inquired, "Are you then acquainted
with my good friend Grylls?"

"I oft to know en, Zur", replied the messenger, "considerin I've
bin sex'on o' the parish for vourteen years, and that me and my fam'ly
have been much beholden to the kindness of the rector both in sickness
and health".

"You are also not without some knowledge of the things related in
this letter. Have you been an eye-witness to any of those strange sights?"

"As var as I'm consarned, Sir, I've been 'pon the road all hours,
night and day and I can zay that I never zeed anything wus than myzelf.
Wan night, tes true my wife and I were awoke by the rattle of wheels,
which was also heered by some of our neighbours, and we all consider'd
that it must be the black coach. But, law, Sir! we have every day such
stories told o'n by creditable people that 'tisn't vur me, a poor plain,
ignorant man to doubt et".

"And how far is the moor from Lanreath?"

"About two miles, and please your reverance. The whole parish is
so frightened that vew will venture far after dummut, vut et hath o' late
come much nigher the church-town. A man who is esteemed a pious and
sensible man by many, though belonging to the Anabaptists, as they be
called, went a few weeks agone to the moor, ('tis called Blackadon),
at midnight vur to lay the sperrit; hes neighbours all axed en to do et;
and he was so frightened at what he zeed that he'th bin nearly mazed
ever since".

"A fitting punishment for his presumption if it hath not quite de-
mented him", said the parson. "These persons are like those addressed
by St. Chrysostom, fitly called the golden mouthed, who said 'Miserable
wretches that ye be! ye cannot expel a flea, much less a devil'. It will be
well if it serves no other purpose but to bring back these stray sheep to
the fold of the church. So this story has gained much belief in your
parish?"

"Most voks believe, as rightly they shud, what hath so many witnesses, though there be zome, young chaps, chiefly, who think they knaw more than their vaathers who won't hear o't though it be sworn to 'pon the Book".

"If those things are disbelieved, friend, and without inquiry, which your disbeliever is ever the first to shrink, of what use is human testimony on any matter? That ghosts have returned to the earth, either for the discovery of murder, or to make restitution for other injustice committed in the flesh, or compelled thereto by the incantations of sorcery, or to communicate tidings from another world, has been testified to in all ages, and many are the instances which have been left to us both in sacred and profane authors. Did not Brutus, when in Asia, as is related by Plutarch see"——

Just at this moment the parson's handmaid said that a person with a hasty message waited on him in the kitchen, or the parson would probably have detailed all those cases in history general and biblical with which his reading had acquainted him; not much we fear to the comfort and edification of the sexton who had to return to Lanreath, a long and dreary road after nightfall. So instead, he directed the girl to take the man with her to the kitchen, and to give him such refreshment as he needed. Meanwhile he wrote to Mr. Grylls telling him that on the next day he had to visit some sick persons in the parish and could not come, but that on the following evening he should be ready to proceed with him to the moor.

On the night appointed the two clergymen left the Lanreath rectory on horseback and reached the moor at ten o'clock. Bleak and dismal did it look by day, but then there was the distant landscape dotted over with pretty homesteads to relieve its desolation. Now, nothing was to be seen but the black patch of sterile moor on which they stood, nothing heard but the wind as it swept in gusts across the bare hill, and howled dismally through a stunted grove of trees that grew in a glen below them, except the occasional baying of dogs from the farm-houses in the distance. That they felt at ease is more than could be expected of them; but as it would have shown a lack of faith in the protection of Heaven which it would have been unseemly in men of their holy calling to exhibit, they managed to conceal from each other their uneasiness. Leading their horses, they trod to and fro through the damp fern and heath with firmness in their steps, and upheld each other by remarks on the power of that Being, whose ministers they were, and the might of whose name they were there to make manifest. Still, slowly and dismally passed the time as they conversed, and anon stopped to look and listen for the approach of their ghostly visitor. In vain. Though the night was as dark and murky as ghost could wish, the coach and its driver came not.

After a considerable stay, the two clergymen consulted together, and determined that it was useless to watch any longer for that night, but that they would meet on some other, when perhaps, it might please his ghostship to appear. Accordingly, with a few words of leave-taking, they separated, Mr. Grylls for the rectory and Mr. Dodge, by a short cut across the moor which shortened his journey by half a mile, for the vicarage of Talland.

The vicar rode on at an ambling pace which his good mare sustained without urging until at the bottom of a valley not far from Blackadon the animal became very uneasy, pricked up her ears, snorted, and moved from side to side of the road as if something stood in the path before her. The parson tightened the reins, and applied whip and spur to her sides, but the horse usually docile, became very unruly, made several attempts to turn, and when prevented threw herself upon her haunches. Whip and spur were applied again and again, to no other purpose than to add to the horses terror. To the rider nothing was apparent which could account for the sudden restiveness of his beast. He dismounted and attempted in turns to lead or drag her, but both were impossible and attended with no small risk of snapping the reins. She was remounted with great difficulty, and yet another unsuccessful attempt made to urge her forward. At length Parson Dodge, judging it to be some special signal from Heaven which it would be dangerous to neglect, threw the reins on the neck of his steed, which wheeling round, started backwards in a direction towards the moor, at a pace which rendered the rider's seat neither a pleasant nor a safe one. In an astonishingly short space of time they were once more on Blackadon.

By this time the bare outline of the moor was broken by a large black group of objects which the darkness prevented Dodge from defining. On approaching this unaccountable appearance the mare was seized with fresh fury, and it was with great difficulty that she could be brought to face this new cause of fright. In the pauses of the mare's prancing the vicar discovered to his horror the much dreaded spectacle of the black coach with its headless steeds, and terrible to relate, his friend, Mr. Grylls, lying prostrate on the ground before the sable driver. Little time was left to him call up his courage for this fearful emergency; for just as the vicar begun to give utterance to the earnest prayer which struggled to his lips, the spectre shouted "Dodge is come! I must be gone!" and forthwith leaped into his chariot, and disappeared across the moor.

The fury of the mare now subsided, and Dodge was enabled to approach his friend who was lying motionless and speechless, with his face buried in the heather.

Meanwhile the rector's horse, which had taken fright at the apparition, and had thrown his rider to the ground on or near the spot where he was found lying, made homeward at a furious speed, and stopped not until he had reached his stable door. The sound of his hoofs as he galloped madly through the village awoke the cottagers, most of whom had been some hours in their beds. Many eager faces, staring with affright, thronged round the rectory, and added by their various conjectures to the fright and apprehensions of the family.

The villagers, gathering courage as their numbers increased, agreed to go in search of the missing clergyman, and started off in a compact body, a few on horseback, but most on foot, for Blackadon. There they found their rector supported in the arms of Parson Dodge, and recovered so far as to be able to speak. Still there was a wildness in his eye, and an incoherency in his speech that shewed that his reason was, at least, temporarily unsettled by the shock. In this condition he was taken to his home followed by his reverend companion.

Here ended this strange adventure; for Mr. Grylls soon completely regained his reason, Parson Dodge got safely back to Talland, and from that time to this nothing has been heard or seen of the black ghost of his chariot.

CIGARETTE CARDS

Smuggling, Pirates and Highwaymen

Published by Ogdens, 1932
50 Smugglers and Smuggling	**15/-**

Published by Lambert and Butler, 1926
25 Pirates and Highwaymen	**4/6**

Published by Carreras, 1924
25 Highwaymen	**13/6**

Published by Paramount Laboratories Ltd., 1957
50 Buccaneers	**3/6**

Old Inns and Taverns

Published by W. D. Wills
40 large cards Old Inns, 1st Series 1936	**27/6**
40 large cards Old Inns, 2nd Series 1939	**15/-**

Published by R. Lloyd
50 standard size Old Inns, 1927	**10/-**

Ships and the Sea

Published by Players
25 Ships Figureheads 1912	**10/6**
25 Ships Figureheads (Large) 1931	**15/-**

Published by Wills, 1925
50 Lighthouses	**7/6**

Published by Hill, 1937
30 Nautical Sons	**6/-**
50 Celebrated Ships	**15/-**

Published by Wills, 1929
25 Rigs of Ships (Large)	**15/-**

Miscellaneous

Published by Wills, 1925
25 Heraldic Signs and their Origins (Large)	**21/-**

Published by Churchman, 1925
25 Curious Signs	**21/-**

Published by Churchman, 1936
50 Legends of Britain	**12/6**

ABOVE PRICES INCLUDE POSTAGE   CASH WITH ORDER

V. GRAHAM, 6, QUEEN'S TERRACE, NEWCASTLE UPON TYNE, 2.

Lindisfarne or Holy Island
Short History and Guide **2/6**

Holy Island
Pictorial Souvenir **2/6**

Holy Island Castle Guide
1/-

Bamburgh and the Farne Islands
2/6

OLD INNS AND TAVERNS
We intend covering the whole of the British Isles with these booklets on a county basis.
All have 48 pages and over 40 illustrations **Price 2/6**

Already Published
Northumberland, Lakeland, 1st and 2nd Series, Cornwall 1st and 2nd Series, Devon 1st Series, Cheshire 1st Series, North Yorkshire.

SMUGGLING
Smuggling in Cornwall **2/6**

Smuggling in Devon **2/6**
All by Frank Graham

Memoirs of a Smuggler **2/6**
by Jack Rattenbury

DICK TURPIN—HIGHWAYMAN
by Charles Harper **2/6**

A BEUK O' NEWCASSEL SONGS
by Joseph Crawhall
First Published in 1888
De Luxe Limited Edition 1965 **30/-**

TYNESIDE SONGS
Compiled by Frank Graham **2/6**

FROM FRANK GRAHAM, 6, QUEEN'S TERRACE, NEWCASTLE UPON TYNE, 2.

BOOKS ON SMUGGLING

SMUGGLING IN CORNWALL
by Frank Graham, 48 pages, illustrated   **2/6**

SMUGGLING IN DEVON
by Frank Graham, 48 pages, illustrated   **2/6**

MEMOIRS OF A SMUGGLER
by Jack Rattenbury, 48 pages, illustrated   **2/6**

CORNISH SMUGGLING TALES
Anthology, Illustrated   **2/6**

OBSERVATIONS, REMARKS and MEANS to PREVENT SMUGGLING
by George Bishop. Maidstone, 1783. Facsimile 24 pages.
Limited edition, 200 copies   **3/6**

SMUGGLERS OF FOWEY
by Commander H. N. Shore, 80 pages, illustrated   **5/-**
                                          Cloth **12/6**

SMUGGLING IN SUSSEX
by William Cooper, 48 pages, illustrated   **2/6**

SMUGGLING IN THE NORTH
by Frank Graham (Covers Yorkshire, Durham, Northumberland) 48 pages, illustrated   **2/6**

SMUGGLING INNS
by Frank Graham, 48 pages, illustrated   **2/6**
Ready Spring 1966.

HISTORY OF POLPERRO
by Jonathan Couch, 96 pages, illustrated. **5/-**. Cloth **12/6**
(Contains a long chapter about the notorious Polperro Smugglers)

Published by
FRANK GRAHAM, 6, QUEEN'S TERRACE, NEWCASTLE UPON TYNE, 2.

SURVEY OF CORNWALL

1584

By JOHN NORDEN

(Called "Speculi Britanniae Pars: A Topographical and Historical Description of Cornwall, with a map of the County and each Hundred")

John Norden was one of the greatest of Elizabethan cartographers. He was born in 1548 and died in 1625. He tried to make a series of county surveys but received no financial support and so the work was not completed. His survey of Cornwall was made in 1584 but not published until 1728.

This book is now very rare and sells at about £50.

Republished for first time on fine paper.

10 Folding maps in facsimile.

Size, Quarto (10½ x 8½ inches). Coloured Cover.

Illustrated by numerous steel engravings.

The earliest and one of the most important surveys of Cornwall.

BOARDS 18/-   CLOTH 30/-

Full Trade Discount

Published by
FRANK GRAHAM, 6, QUEEN'S TERRACE, NEWCASTLE UPON TYNE, 2.

Old Books, Prints and Maps

VERA GRAHAM

6 QUEEN'S TERRACE, NEWCASTLE UPON TYNE, 2

The largest antiquarian print and map dealer in the north of England is always interested in buying all topographical books, over 100 years old and collections of old maps.

FOLLOWING BOOKS ALWAYS WANTED

BESLEY—Devon and Cornwall
ALLOM—Devon and Cornwall
SHEPHERD'S Edinburgh
SWARBRECK'S Scotland
ALLEN'S Yorkshire
HARWOOD'S English Scenery
WRIGHT'S Essex
RITCHIE'S Windsor
BRITTON—English Cities
MAYHEW—The Rhine
TOMBLESON—The Thames
TOMBLESON—The Rhine
SHEPHERD'S London
MOULE—English Counties
ROMNEY—Chester and its
  Environs

BATENHAM—Street Views
  Chester
ALLOM—Derby and Chester
PROUT—Antiquities of Chester
BRAND—History of Newcastle
MACKENZIE—History of
  Newcastle
COLLARD—Views of Newcastle
MUDIE'S Hampshire
ALLOM—Northumberland,
  Durham, Cumberland
NUTTER—Carlisle in Olden
  Time
BILLING'S Durham
SHEPHERD—Bath and Bristol
TALLIS—Illustrated Atlas

SPECIALIST IN OLD ENGRAVINGS OF TOWNS AND SCENES IN EVERY PART OF THE BRITISH ISLES AND THE CONTINENT

Printed by Howe Brothers (Gateshead) Limited